THE POWER OF AI FOR EDUCATORS

REVOLUTIONIZE TEACHING TO STAY COMPETITIVE, DRAMATICALLY REDUCE WORKLOAD, AND PERSONALIZE LEARNING TO INCREASE STUDENT ENGAGEMENT AND MOTIVATION.

VICTORIA R. SUMMERS

TABLE OF CONTENTS

INTRODUCTION

In the very near future, envision a classroom where learning is deeply personalized, where each student's educational journey is meticulously crafted to align with their strengths, needs, and interests, all thanks to artificial intelligence. In this setting, educators effortlessly facilitate a landscape of personalized learning; students are more than just attentive —they are profoundly engaged and motivated by a curriculum that seems tailor-made.

My journey into exploring AI and education began with a simple observation: technology is not just a tool but a transformative element that can fundamentally enhance how we teach and learn. As an advocate for technological integration in education, I've dedicated my career to exploring innovative ways to bring AI into classrooms. My passion for this venture stems from a commitment to not only understanding these technologies but also ensuring they serve as bridges rather than barriers in educational settings.

This book is born out of a vision to demystify the power of AI in transforming education. It is designed to guide you through the extensive ways that AI can revolutionize classroom experiences, address current and emerging challenges such as academic dishonesty, and cater to students' diverse learning needs. My goal is to equip you with practical strategies for integrating AI tools into your teaching practices while also navigating the ethical landscapes that accompany new technologies.

Through this work, I aim to provide a unique blend of practical advice backed by the latest research and my own experiences in the field. You'll find insights into innovative teaching methods that leverage AI to enhance learning outcomes and make educational content more engaging and relevant. Moreover, this book will provide insights into the latest advancements in AI, ensuring you're always at the cutting edge of educational technology.

The importance of staying technologically informed cannot be overstated, especially in education. AI is not just about automation or efficiency; it's about preparing our students for a future where AI is ubiquitous. This book will explore how embracing AI in education today can cultivate the skills and mindsets that will be crucial tomorrow.

Structured to serve as both a guide and a companion, the chapters ahead will walk you through practical applications and ethical considerations and anticipate future trends in AI in education. Alongside startling statistics—like the prediction that AI could nearly double the rate of innovation and learning effectiveness in educational settings by 2030—this book underscores the urgency and relevance of integrating AI into your teaching repertoire.

Reflecting on a recent classroom success story, where a once disengaged student found new joy in learning through AI-driven personalization, I'm reminded daily why I embarked on this path. Stories like these fuel my passion and drive to spread the word about AI's potential in education.

Join me on this explorative journey to unlock the transformative power of AI in your teaching practices. Together, let's prepare to meet the future of education head-on, equipped with knowledge, strategies, and an unwavering commitment to our students' success.

1

UNDERSTANDING AI IN EDUCATION

As educators, you continually seek tools that not only simplify teaching tasks but profoundly enrich the learning experience for your students. The advent of Artificial Intelligence (AI) in education offers unprecedented opportunities to achieve these goals. However, the complexity and rapid evolution of AI can often seem daunting. This chapter aims to demystify AI for you, providing a clear understanding of its definitions, types, capabilities, and its invaluable role in modern educational environments. By embracing AI, you can enhance personalized learning experiences and administrative efficiency, ensuring your students are well-prepared for the future.

1.1 WHAT IS AI? DEMYSTIFYING THE TECHNOLOGY FOR EDUCATORS

Artificial Intelligence, or AI, is the simulation of human intelligence in machines programmed to think like humans and mimic their actions. The term may also be applied to any machine that exhibits traits associated with a human mind, such as learning and problem-solving. The ideal characteristic of AI is its ability to rationalize and take actions that have the best chance of achieving a specific goal. A subset of AI is machine learning, which refers to the concept that computer programs can automatically learn from and adapt to new data without being assisted by humans. Deep learning techniques enable this automatic learning by absorbing vast amounts of unstructured data such as text, images, or video.

AI technologies come in several forms, each of which may have distinct applications in educational settings. First, reactive machines are basic AI systems that operate based solely on the current data, taking into account only the current situation. IBM's chess-playing Deep Blue, which beat international grandmaster Garry Kasparov in the late 1990s, is an example of this type of machine. Next, limited memory AI can make informed and improved decisions by studying past data from its memory. Such AI is commonly used in autonomous vehicles but can be applied in educational settings to adapt learning based on students' past behaviors.

More advanced are the theory of mind and self-aware AI types, which are still in experimental stages but hold intriguing educational implications. Theory of mind AI aims to understand better the entities it interacts with by discerning their needs, emotions, beliefs, and thought processes. Although fully developed AI of this kind is not yet a reality, its prospects include creating more responsive learning environments that adapt to the emotional state of students. Self-aware AI, an extension of the theory of mind, is designed to have consciousness, sentiments, and self-awareness. While self-aware AI might sound like science fiction, it prompts educators to ponder profound questions about the role of technology in teaching and learning.

Despite its capabilities, AI does not come without misunderstandings. It's crucial to clarify that AI does not function autonomously in educational settings. The fear that AI might replace teachers is unfounded; instead, AI should be seen as a powerful tool to assist and enhance the teaching process. AI systems require human oversight to function effectively, especially in complex, ever-changing environments like classrooms. They are designed to handle tasks that can optimize workflow, personalize learning, and manage time-consuming administrative duties, allowing teachers more time to focus on the pedagogical approaches that require a human touch.

AI's role in education is transformative, offering tailored learning experiences and operational efficiencies that were previously difficult or impossible to achieve. It enables personalized education at scale, where every student can learn at their own pace and style. It also gives teachers actionable insights into students' learning patterns and needs. Moreover, AI can automate routine tasks such as grading and attendance, freeing educators to engage more deeply with their students. As we continue to integrate AI into educational spaces, it is imperative to approach this technology as an ally in enhancing educational outcomes and preparing students for a future where AI will undoubtedly be a ubiquitous presence.

1.2 THE EVOLUTION OF AI IN EDUCATIONAL TOOLS AND PLATFORMS

The evolution of artificial intelligence (AI) has profoundly shaped the landscape of education, with each technological milestone marking new possibilities for enhancing teaching and learning. Tracing the trajectory of AI's development offers invaluable insights into how these technologies have come to play a pivotal role in education today.

The genesis of AI in education can be traced back to the 1960s with the introduction of programmed learning and computer-assisted instruction. These early forms of educational technology were primitive by today's standards but marked the beginning of using machine assistance to deliver educational content. Systems such as PLATO (Programmed Logic for Automatic Teaching Operations) represented initial efforts to integrate computing power in academic settings, providing students with drills, quizzes, and basic simulations. The evolution continued through the 1970s and 1980s as more sophisticated programmed learning tools were developed, laying the groundwork for the more personalized and adaptive technologies that would emerge later.

The fundamental transformation in educational AI began to accelerate with the advent of the internet and the increasing computational power of personal computers in the late 1990s and early 2000s. This period saw the development of more sophisticated educational software that could adapt to the individual learning pace of students, a practice known as adaptive learning. Systems like Cognitive Tutor, developed in the late 1990s, used complex algorithms to tailor content to the student's learning needs, providing real-time feedback and personalized instruction paths. This adaptability was a significant step forward in creating more individualized learning experiences that could accommodate students' varying levels of understanding and learning speeds.

In recent years, the integration of advanced AI technologies like machine learning and natural language processing has further transformed educational platforms. Today's AI-powered educational tools are capable of analyzing vast amounts of data from student interactions and generating insights that were previously impossible to obtain. For instance, machine learning algorithms now underpin platforms that can predict student performance, identify at-risk students, and recommend interventions tailored to individual learning profiles. Additionally, natural language processing has enabled the creation of sophisticated AI tutors that can converse with students in natural language, help solve their queries, and provide explanations for complex concepts, thereby enriching the learning experience.

The impact of these technologies on teaching and learning has been profound. AI has transformed how content is delivered and consumed and reshaped the roles of teachers and learners. Educators can now focus more on facilitating learning than providing information as AI takes on more administrative burdens and routine educational tasks. This shift has allowed teachers to spend more time on higher-order teaching tasks such as critical thinking, problem-solving, and emotional support, which are essential for comprehensive education but often sidelined due to time constraints. For students, AI has opened up new avenues for personalized learning, providing platforms that adapt to their learning styles and speeds, thus making education more inclusive and effective.

Moreover, the use of AI in education has democratized learning in significant ways. Students from various socio-economic backgrounds can access high-quality personalized education that was once only available to the privileged few. This democratization is particularly impactful in regions where educational resources are scarce, as AI-powered educational tools can provide high-quality learning experiences without requiring extensive physical infrastructure.

As we look to the future, the ongoing integration of AI in educational tools and platforms promises even more revolutionary changes to the academic landscape. With continual advancements in AI technology, the potential for creating more adaptive, responsive, and personalized learning environments is boundless. Educators and students alike stand to benefit immensely as these tools become more refined and accessible, offering prospects for a more equitable, effective, and engaging educational experience worldwide.

1.3 KEY AI CONCEPTS EVERY EDUCATOR SHOULD KNOW

Grasping the core concepts of Artificial Intelligence (AI) is pivotal for educators aiming to integrate this technology effectively into their teaching environments. AI is reshaping educational landscapes, and understanding its fundamental aspects can significantly enhance teaching and learning experiences. Let's explore some critical AI concepts that every educator should be familiar with, focusing on how these can be practically applied within educational settings.

Machine learning is a cornerstone of AI, especially in educational applications. At its core, machine learning is a branch of AI that allows systems to learn from data, identify patterns, and make decisions with minimal human intervention. Its significance in educational tools lies in its ability to adapt learning experiences to the needs of individual students. For instance, adaptive learning systems use machine-saving techniques to analyze student responses. Based on this analysis, the system adjusts the difficulty and type of content presented, ensuring that each student receives a personalized learning experience that is relatively easy and manageable. This dynamic adjustment helps maintain students' interest and promotes effective learning by constantly challenging them just enough to keep them engaged without causing frustration.

Natural Language Processing (NLP) is another transformative AI concept that enables computers to understand, interpret, and respond to human language in a meaningful and helpful way. In educational contexts, NLP can power AI tutors and chatbots, which provide real-time, on-demand academic support. NLP-driven chatbots can converse with students in natural language, offering explanations, guiding them through complex problems, or providing feedback on their work. For example, an AI tutor powered by NLP might assist a student struggling with grammar by offering tailored examples and interactive exercises that target the student's specific difficulties. This immediate, personalized feedback can help clarify misunderstandings and reinforce learning, enhancing educational outcomes.

Inspired by the biological neural networks that constitute animal brains, neural networks play a crucial role in many AI applications, including those in education. Essentially, neural networks are algorithms designed to recognize patterns by interpreting data through a structure that mimics the human brain's interconnected neuron structure. This capability makes them particularly useful in personalized learning analytics. For instance, neural networks can analyze how students interact with an e-learning platform, identifying patterns that may indicate a student's preferred learning pace or potential difficulties with specific concepts. By recognizing these patterns, educational software can adapt in real-time to the needs of each student, providing a truly customized academic experience that optimizes learning efficiency and effectiveness.

Data mining, the process of discovering patterns and extracting information from large datasets, is integral to the functioning of AI in education. Through data mining, educational platforms can uncover insights about learning behaviors and outcomes that would be difficult, if not impossible, for humans to detect without technological assistance. These insights can then inform educational strategies and interventions. For example, by analyzing data from thousands of students, an educational platform might identify that students participating in certain interactive activities are more likely to understand and retain complex scientific concepts. With this knowledge, educators can design more effective curricula incorporating these successful strategies, enhancing learning outcomes.

Understanding these key AI concepts allows educators to better grasp how AI tools operate and their potential for transforming educational practices. By integrating AI-driven technologies such as machine learning, NLP, neural networks, and data mining into academic settings, educators can provide highly personalized, engaging, and effective learning experiences for all students. As AI continues to evolve, staying informed about these fundamental concepts will enable educators to remain at the forefront of educational innovation, ensuring they can meet the diverse needs of their students in an increasingly digital world.

1.4 COMPARING AI TECHNOLOGIES: WHICH FITS YOUR CLASSROOM?

Selecting the appropriate AI technology for educational settings involves a nuanced understanding of the tools available and the specific needs of your classroom. As educators, integrating AI into your teaching practices should begin with a rigorous assessment of these needs to ensure that the chosen technology effectively supports your educational objectives and enhances learning outcomes.

Assessment of Needs

The initial step in this process involves a detailed assessment of classroom needs. This includes identifying areas where students are struggling, where teacher workloads can be streamlined, and where engagement can be enhanced. For instance, if students struggle with personalized feedback in large classes, AI technologies that offer real-time feedback might be considered. Similarly, if administrative tasks such as grading consume significant classroom time, AI solutions that automate these processes could be beneficial.

Conducting surveys, observing classroom interactions, and analyzing performance data can provide valuable insights into these needs, guiding the selection of AI tools.

Matching AI Tools to Educational Goals

Once classroom needs are understood, the next step is to match them with specific AI tools designed to meet them. Selecting AI technologies based on clear criteria that align with your educational goals is crucial. For example, if enhancing student engagement is a priority, AI tools that incorporate gamification elements or interactive content might be appropriate. Alternatively, AI systems equipped with adaptive learning technologies could be more suitable if the goal is to provide differentiated learning paths. Each tool should be evaluated on its ability to meet specific educational outcomes, ease of integration into existing systems, and user-friendliness for students and teachers.

Examples of AI Integration

To illustrate the practical applications of AI in educational settings, consider the case of a high school in Sweden that implemented an AI-driven platform to enhance language learning. The platform used machine learning algorithms to adaptively assess each student's language capabilities and tailor exercises to their level. This personalized approach helped students progress at their own pace and significantly improved language proficiency across the classroom. Another example is a university in Japan that used AI to analyze student submission patterns and predict potential dropouts. By identifying at-risk students early, the institution was able to intervene more effectively and improve retention rates. These examples demonstrate how AI can strategically address educational challenges and enhance learning outcomes.

Considerations for Integration

Integrating AI into educational environments requires careful consideration of logistical, ethical, and pedagogical factors. Logistically, the availability of resources such as hardware, internet connectivity, and technical support must be assessed. Ethically, it is essential to consider how student data will be used and protected, ensuring compliance with data protection regulations and maintaining transparency with stakeholders. Pedagogically, educators must consider how AI will impact teaching dynamics and student interactions. Training teachers on effectively using and integrating AI tools is crucial, as is ongoing support for adapting these tools to evolving educational needs.

Educators can make informed decisions about implementing AI technologies by thoroughly assessing classroom needs, carefully selecting AI tools that align with educational goals, examining practical examples of AI integration, and considering all logistical, ethical, and pedagogical factors. This strategic approach ensures that AI is a powerful ally in enhancing educational outcomes and preparing students for a future in which technology and learning are inextricably linked.

1.5 DEBUNKING MYTHS: WHAT AI CAN AND CANNOT DO IN EDUCATION

When discussing Artificial Intelligence in the context of education, it is crucial to separate factual capabilities from fictional speculation. AI, while a groundbreaking tool potentially transforming educational landscapes, is not a panacea for all educational challenges nor a threat to the teaching profession. It is a technology designed to augment and enhance teaching and learning processes through specific, well-defined functionalities. Understanding what AI can realistically achieve helps set appropriate expectations and fosters an environment where integration into educational settings can be genuinely beneficial.

AI's capabilities within education are numerous and significant. For instance, AI can automate administrative tasks such as grading and attendance tracking, reducing the workload on educators and allowing them more time to focus on student interaction and pedagogical refinement. In terms of personalized learning, AI excels by analyzing large datasets to adapt the learning content to the needs of individual students, thereby catering to diverse learning speeds and styles. However, AI's ability to completely replace a teacher's nuanced, empathetic, and motivational role is still firmly within science fiction. AI does not possess human-like consciousness and cannot replicate the complex human interactions crucial in educational settings. Teachers' roles are evolving into technology facilitators rather than being replaced by them, guiding students in using AI as a learning tool.

Moreover, the hype surrounding AI can sometimes lead to unrealistic expectations. While AI can provide data-driven insights and recommendations, it is not infallible. The output quality of AI depends heavily on the input it receives, which means that data biases or errors can lead to less effective or even misleading recommendations. Educators must understand the importance of maintaining a critical eye on the information provided by AI systems. They should integrate these tools to complement traditional teaching methods rather than depending entirely on them. Realistic expectations about what AI can achieve in the classroom can prevent disappointment and optimize the technology's practical benefits.

Ethical considerations also play a critical role in defining the boundaries of AI's capabilities in educational settings. Issues surrounding data privacy are paramount, as the use of AI involves the processing and storage of sensitive student information. Ensuring this data is handled securely and complies with regulations such as the General Data Protection Regulation (GDPR) is essential. Furthermore, the risk of bias in AI algorithms, manifesting in the tools used for assessments or admissions, must be diligently addressed. Educators and developers alike must strive to create and implement AI systems that are as unbiased as possible and transparent in their operations, ensuring fairness and equity in educational outcomes.

Looking to the future, the possibilities for AI in education are expanding as technology advances. Ongoing research in AI promises even more sophisticated tools that could further personalize learning and make educational resources more accessible to underserved populations. For example, advancements in AI could lead to more effective language translation tools, breaking down barriers for non-native speakers and allowing for genuinely global classrooms. Additionally, AI might soon provide simulations and virtual reality experiences that offer students immersive and interactive learning environments, regardless of geographical location. These future capabilities, grounded in current trends and research, suggest a bright horizon for AI in education, provided these tools are used responsibly and ethically.

In conclusion, as we navigate the complexities of AI in educational contexts, it is essential to maintain a clear and informed perspective on what AI can and cannot achieve. By debunking myths and setting realistic expectations, educators can leverage AI as a powerful ally in enhancing educational outcomes and preparing students for a future where technology and learning go hand in hand.

1.6 THE ROLE OF DATA IN AI: UNDERSTANDING DATA PRIVACY AND ETHICS

In educational AI, data is the foundational element that fuels the intelligence of these systems. AI's capacity to enhance and personalize the educational experience heavily relies on data. This data can range from student demographic information and learning progress records to more detailed interactions within educational software, such as quiz responses, assignment submissions, and social interactions in learning management systems. Each piece of data helps to paint a more detailed picture of a student's learning journey, allowing AI systems to adjust and tailor educational experiences to meet individual student needs effectively.

However, the reliance on data ushers in significant concerns regarding privacy and the ethical handling of this information. As educators, it is paramount to understand and address these concerns to maintain the trust of students and their families. Regulations such as the General Data Protection Regulation (GDPR) in the European Union and the Family Educational Rights and Privacy Act (FERPA) in the United States provide frameworks to ensure student data is handled securely and privately. These regulations enforce strict data storage, access, and processing guidelines, ensuring educational institutions and tech providers adhere to the highest data protection standards.

Beyond compliance with legal requirements, the ethical use of AI in education encompasses a broader spectrum of considerations. Transparency in how AI systems use student data is crucial. Educators and technology providers must be transparent about what data is being collected, how it is being used, and who has access to it. This transparency is essential not only for compliance with regulations but also for gaining and maintaining the trust of students and parents. Furthermore, accountability in AI-driven decisions is a critical ethical concern. Decisions made by AI, such as student evaluations or recommendations for course placements, can significantly impact a student's educational trajectory. As such, mechanisms must be in place to review and challenge AI decisions, ensuring they are fair and just.

Fairness in AI is another ethical cornerstone that must be rigorously upheld. Like any technology, AI systems can inadvertently become biased based on the data they are fed. For instance, if an AI-based assessment tool is trained predominantly with data from a specific demographic, it may perform less effectively for students outside that demographic. To combat this, AI systems used in education must be continuously monitored and updated to address potential biases, ensuring that all students are assessed and treated fairly. This commitment to fairness enhances the effectiveness of educational AI and upholds the ethical standards expected in academic environments.

To navigate these complex landscapes of data privacy and ethics effectively, educators should adhere to several best practices for data management. First, understanding and staying informed about the relevant privacy laws and ethical guidelines is crucial. Regular training sessions on data protection regulations and ethical AI use can help educators remain knowledgeable and compliant. Secondly, educators should prioritize selecting vendors who commit to ethical AI practices when implementing AI tools. This includes clear policies on data usage, robust security measures, and transparency in their operations.

Another best practice is implementing strict access controls and data encryption to protect student information from unauthorized access. Additionally, educators should foster open communication with students and parents about the AI tools being used and the measures taken to protect student data. This openness helps build trust and allows for a more receptive attitude towards using AI in education.

Lastly, maintaining an active collaboration between educators, AI technicians, and ethicists can ensure that AI systems are used responsibly. This collaborative approach allows for continuously re-evaluating AI tools and strategies, ensuring they remain aligned with educational goals and ethical standards. By following these guidelines, educators can harness the benefits of AI in education while safeguarding the privacy and rights of students, paving the way for a more informed, ethical, and effective use of technology in educational settings.

2

PRACTICAL AI APPLICATIONS IN THE CLASSROOM

As you delve deeper into the transformative world of AI in education, the focus shifts from understanding its foundational concepts to exploring practical applications that can truly revolutionize the way you teach. This chapter demonstrates how, when thoughtfully integrated, AI tools can create personalized, dynamic, and responsive learning environments that uniquely cater to every student's needs. AI transcends theoretical discussions, manifesting in real-world applications that underscore its profound impact on personalized education.

2.1 INTEGRATING AI TOOLS FOR PERSONALIZED LEARNING PATHS

Identifying Student Needs

The cornerstone of effective education lies in accurately identifying and addressing the unique needs of each student. AI excels in this area by leveraging data analytics to decipher various patterns in student performance and engagement. Imagine AI systems as diligent assistants that process vast amounts of data—from test scores and homework completion rates to interactive session feedback. These systems use advanced algorithms to detect individual strengths, weaknesses, and learning preferences. By analyzing this data, AI tools can identify specific educational needs at a personal level, allowing you to tailor your teaching strategies accordingly. For instance, if AI analytics reveal that a student excels in visual learning but struggles with textual information, this insight allows you to adjust your content delivery to include more diagrams, videos, and infographics, thus enhancing the student's comprehension and engagement.

Customizing Learning Materials

With the insights gained from AI-driven analytics, the next step involves customizing learning materials to suit your students' diverse learning paces and styles. AI's capability to automate the customization process ensures efficiency and guarantees a level of personalization that is difficult to achieve manually. AI-powered educational platforms can dynamically generate and adapt learning content based on real-time performance data. For example, if a student demonstrates quick mastery of a concept, the AI system can immediately introduce more advanced materials to maintain a challenging learning environment. Conversely, if a student struggles with a particular topic, the system can provide remedial content to reinforce foundational concepts, ensuring no student is left behind.

Continuous Feedback Loop

AI systems facilitate a continuous feedback loop, a critical component in a dynamic learning environment. These systems provide real-time feedback to students and educators, enabling immediate adjustments and fostering an adaptive learning atmosphere. For students, immediate feedback on assignments and quizzes allows them to understand their mistakes and learn from them promptly, thus enhancing learning efficacy. For you, as an educator, the feedback from AI systems on student performance and engagement can guide your teaching strategy. This ongoing loop of feedback and adaptation ensures that the learning process remains responsive and effectively aligned with the students' evolving educational needs.

Case Studies

Several schools globally have begun recognizing and harnessing AI's benefits in creating personalized learning paths. A notable example is a middle school in California, where AI systems have been implemented effectively. The school uses AI to analyze students' learning habits and tailor homework and in-class activities to suit individual learning speeds. This approach has improved academic performance, student engagement, and satisfaction.

Another example comes from a high school in Finland, where AI-driven platforms provide personalized learning experiences in mathematics. The system tracks each student's progress and adapts the difficulty of problems and the pace of the curriculum accordingly. Teachers report that this personalized approach has led to higher student motivation and a deeper understanding of complex mathematical concepts.

These examples highlight the practical benefits of integrating AI tools into education, demonstrating how they can transform traditional learning environments into engaging, personalized educational experiences. As AI continues to evolve, its role in education will undoubtedly expand, offering even more innovative ways to meet the diverse needs of students worldwide.

2.2 AI AND THE FLIPPED CLASSROOM: A PRACTICAL GUIDE

In the evolving landscape of educational methodologies, the flipped classroom model stands out for its innovative approach to learning and teaching. This model reverses the traditional learning environment by delivering instructional content, often online, outside the classroom. It moves activities into the classroom, including those that may have traditionally been considered homework. AI's role in enhancing this model is pivotal, as it offers tools that can curate and customize instructional content for students to study at home, thus maximizing classroom interaction and deepening learning experiences.

AI's capability to personalize pre-class learning materials based on the individual learning progress of each student is invaluable in a flipped classroom setting. Using sophisticated algorithms, AI can analyze previous performance data to tailor the educational content each student accesses at home. For instance, if a student demonstrates proficiency in a particular topic, AI can adjust to present more challenging content or delve deeper into complex aspects of the subject. Conversely, AI can recalibrate the available content for topics where a student may need help reinforcing foundational concepts, ensuring the student stays caught up. This personalized approach ensures that each student comes to class prepared and at a relatively uniform level of readiness, which is critical for the success of in-class activities.

Once in the classroom, AI continues to support educators by helping to design more effective in-class activities. With insights from data on students' home learning progress, AI tools can suggest or generate activities that reinforce or expand on those topics. For example, suppose the AI system identifies that many students struggled with a particular concept in their pre-class assignments. In that case, it can suggest specific in-class activities or group discussions to address these challenges. This ensures that classroom time is used effectively, focusing on areas requiring further clarification and enhancing the learning process.

Moreover, AI is crucial in providing continuous feedback and suggesting adjustments to students and educators. By continuously analyzing data on how students interact with both home-study materials and in-class activities, AI can provide real-time feedback to educators about the effectiveness of their flipped classroom strategies. This might include insights into how well different pre-class materials prepare students for in-class activities or how different in-class strategies contribute to student learning outcomes. Armed with this information, educators can make informed adjustments to their teaching methods and materials, continually refining the learning process to meet the needs of their students better.

When considering the implementation of AI in a flipped classroom model, several tools and platforms stand out for their robust capabilities and proven effectiveness. Platforms like Knewton provide adaptive learning technologies that tailor pre-class instructional content to the needs of individual students, enhancing their preparedness for class. Another powerful tool, Classkick, allows educators to create interactive assignments that students can complete independently, providing immediate feedback and allowing peers and teachers to offer real-time help before class. These tools exemplify how AI can support the flipped classroom model, making learning more personalized, interactive, and effective.

As AI advances, its integration into educational models like the flipped classroom will likely become more sophisticated, offering even greater support for personalized learning and efficient classroom management. This ongoing evolution promises to enhance the effectiveness of educational environments further, preparing students more effectively for the complexities of the modern world.

2.3 USING AI TO ENHANCE STUDENT ASSESSMENTS

Assessment is critical in measuring student progress, determining academic success, and shaping future educational instructional strategies. With the integration of Artificial Intelligence, the approach to student assessments is undergoing a significant transformation. AI brings sophistication to the evaluation process, making it not only faster but also more adaptive and far-reaching in its ability to ensure academic integrity and predict student outcomes.

Automated Grading

One of the most immediate benefits of AI in educational assessments is automated grading. This AI capability particularly applies to objective assessments, which include formats such as multiple-choice questions, fill-in-the-blanks, and true or false questions. By automating the grading process, AI systems can swiftly analyze large volumes of student responses with high accuracy. This efficiency frees you, the educator, from the time-consuming task of grading such assessments manually. Consequently, this allows you more time to focus on providing qualitative feedback on subjective assessments, where human judgment and interaction are crucial. For example, while AI efficiently handles the grading of a science quiz, you can dedicate more attention to providing personalized feedback on essays or project-based assignments, which are instrumental in developing students' critical thinking and creative skills.

Furthermore, integrating AI in grading enhances efficiency and ensures objectivity in scoring. Human graders can unintentionally bring personal biases into the grading process. AI systems, programmed to follow strict answer keys and rubrics, eliminate this variability, providing a consistent and fair grading standard that students can trust. This objectivity is crucial in maintaining transparency and fairness in educational evaluations, contributing to a more equitable learning environment.

Adaptive Assessments

Adaptive assessments stand as a hallmark of how AI can revolutionize educational evaluations. Unlike traditional assessments, which are static and uniform for all students, adaptive assessments designed by AI dynamically adjust their difficulty based on a student's performance. If a student answers a question correctly, the AI system presents a more challenging question. Conversely, if a student struggles with a question, the subsequent one will be easier. This approach not only tailors the assessment to the individual's learning level but also keeps students neither overly challenged nor under-stimulated.

The benefits of adaptive assessments are profound. They provide a more accurate measure of a student's abilities and knowledge, free from the constraints of a one-size-fits-all test. Additionally, these assessments can help identify specific areas where a student might need further improvement, allowing for targeted interventions that are more likely to improve learning outcomes. Moreover, adaptive assessments can enhance student engagement and motivation, as students are more likely to stay engaged with tasks within their zone of proximal development—the sweet spot where the task is neither too challenging nor too easy, which Vygotsky identified as crucial for cognitive development.

Plagiarism and Integrity Checks

Academic integrity is a cornerstone of educational institutions, and AI's role in upholding this principle is increasingly vital. AI-powered tools can now scan student submissions and compare them against vast databases of existing work to detect similarities that may indicate plagiarism. These tools extend beyond simple text comparisons; they can analyze the semantics and paraphrasing efforts that might otherwise slip past more basic plagiarism checkers.

Moreover, AI systems are being trained to detect other forms of academic dishonesty, such as contract cheating, where students submit work done by others as their own. By flagging stylistic inconsistencies in writing or unusual patterns in code (in the case of programming assignments), AI tools can alert educators to potential misconduct. This capability is crucial for ensuring fairness and equity in academic evaluations and teaching students the importance of academic honesty and the consequences of unethical behavior.

Predictive Analytics

Lastly, applying predictive analytics in education illustrates AI's capacity to assess what has been learned and anticipate future outcomes. AI systems analyze patterns in assessment data to predict student performance, providing insights that can preemptively identify students at risk of underperforming. This proactive approach allows for timely interventions, such as additional tutoring, tailored homework, or other support mechanisms, which can be crucial in helping students stay on track.

Predictive analytics also play a role in curriculum development. By identifying which parts of the course students tend to struggle with, educators can adjust the curriculum to address these difficulties, enhancing the overall effectiveness of educational programs. This foresight enables a more responsive education system that adapts to meet students' evolving needs and prepares them for future challenges.

By harnessing AI in these diverse aspects of student assessments, educators can enhance educational evaluations' efficiency, fairness, and effectiveness. This transformation supports academic integrity and personalized learning and fosters an environment where students are equipped to achieve their best possible outcomes.

2.4 AI-POWERED GAME-BASED LEARNING TECHNIQUES

The convergence of game-based learning and artificial intelligence marks a transformative era in educational methodologies, where engagement and personalization are at the forefront of student interaction. Utilizing AI to gamify learning experiences captures students' attention and significantly enhances their motivation and engagement. This approach leverages the intrinsic human affinity for games to foster a deeper connection with educational content. AI-driven gamification introduces elements such as points, levels, and challenges into the learning process, mirroring the engaging aspects of video games. These elements effectively motivate students, providing a sense of accomplishment and progress. For example, an AI system can integrate game mechanics into a math teaching tool, where students earn badges for mastering new concepts or improving their speed and accuracy in solving problems. This makes the learning process more engaging and encourages healthy competition and a continuous desire for improvement among students.

Moreover, the personalization capabilities of AI significantly enhance the efficacy of game-based learning. AI-driven educational games adapt in real-time to each student's learning pace and style, ensuring the academic content is manageable. This adaptive learning environment is achieved through sophisticated algorithms that analyze each student's interactions and performance within the game. Depending on a student's responses, the AI dynamically adjusts the tasks' difficulty, the questions' complexity, and even the type of content presented, ensuring a tailored learning experience that maximizes engagement and effectiveness. For instance, if a student excels in numerical reasoning but struggles with geometric concepts, the AI can modify the game to incorporate more geometric challenges presented in a way that aligns with the student's learning preferences, such as through visual puzzles or interactive diagrams.

Assessment within these AI-powered games is another area where the capabilities of AI are leveraged to enhance learning outcomes. Unlike traditional assessments, which might occur at the end of a learning unit, AI-enabled games assess students' understanding continuously as they interact with the game. This method provides immediate feedback to students, allowing for quick correction of misconceptions and reinforcing continuous learning throughout the gameplay. Additionally, this constant assessment offers educators a wealth of data about each student's learning progress, areas of strength, and potential weaknesses. This information is invaluable for informing future teaching strategies and providing targeted support to students needing extra help.

The effectiveness of AI-powered game-based learning is not just theoretical but is supported by numerous successful implementations across various educational settings. For example, a game developed for middle school science students uses AI to guide students through a series of experiments in a virtual laboratory. As students interact with different elements in the lab, the AI provides feedback and adjusts the complexity of the experiments based on the student's performance. This dynamic interaction engages students and makes learning science concepts more accessible and enjoyable. Another notable example is an AI-driven language learning game that adapts to the user's proficiency level. The game includes a variety of interactive scenarios that simulate real-life conversations, with the AI adjusting the difficulty of the dialogue and the vocabulary based on the user's responses. This personalized approach helps students build their language skills more effectively and maintains their interest in learning.

These examples underscore the potential of AI-powered game-based learning to transform educational experiences, making them more engaging, personalized, and effective. As AI technology continues to evolve, the possibilities for its application in educational gaming are bound to expand, opening up new avenues for enhancing learning and teaching across the globe. This integration of AI in game-based learning supports students' academic development and prepares them to navigate an increasingly digital world where technology and learning go hand in hand.

2.5 AUTOMATING ADMINISTRATIVE TASKS WITH AI TO FOCUS ON TEACHING

The administrative demands on educators can often be overwhelming, detracting from the core mission of teaching and directly engaging with students. Fortunately, AI technology offers substantial capabilities in automating routine administrative tasks that are essential yet time-consuming. By integrating AI into these processes, you, as an educator, can reclaim valuable time to focus more on pedagogical activities and less on administrative duties.

One of the most common areas where AI can play a transformative role is automating mundane tasks such as attendance taking, grade recording, and scheduling. AI-driven systems can efficiently manage daily attendance, instantly noting which students are present, tardy, or absent without any manual input from teachers. This data is automatically updated in the school's records system, ensuring accuracy and immediacy. Similarly, AI can automate the recording of grades into electronic grade books. As assessments are completed and graded, AI systems can input these grades into the relevant databases, significantly reducing the potential for human error and the time spent on manual entries. Furthermore, AI can oversee scheduling tasks, from arranging parent-teacher conferences based on teacher and parent availability to optimizing class schedules to ensure efficient use of resources and facilities. This level of automation streamlines administrative operations and enhances organizational efficiency, allowing schools to operate more smoothly.

In communication, AI has introduced sophisticated chatbots that can handle routine interactions with students and parents, freeing up significant time. These AI chatbots are programmed to respond to common inquiries about homework assignments, project deadlines, exam schedules, and school events, providing timely and accurate information. More advanced AI systems can send reminders for upcoming assignments or meetings, ensuring all parties are well-informed without requiring direct teacher involvement. This capability enhances communication efficiency and ensures that you can dedicate more attention to preparing lessons and supporting students rather than managing logistical queries.

Moreover, AI's impact extends into data analysis and reporting, which is crucial for informed educational management decision-making. AI systems can aggregate and analyze vast amounts of academic data, from student performance to resource utilization, providing insights that can guide school management decisions. For instance, AI can highlight trends in student performance across different subjects, identifying areas where the curriculum may need adjustment. It can also monitor resource allocation, suggesting optimal use of materials and facilities based on actual usage patterns. These insights are often synthesized in detailed reports generated by AI, which support daily management tasks and strategic planning activities. The ability of AI to handle these complex data analysis tasks not only supports more informed decision-making but also significantly reduces the workload involved in manual data handling and report generation.

The impact of AI-driven automation on teacher workload cannot be overstated. Numerous studies and reports have highlighted how integrating AI into administrative tasks can substantially reduce teachers' time on non-teaching activities. For example, research indicates that AI automation can save teachers up to 20-30% of their time by handling routine administrative tasks. This can then be redirected towards more interactive and student-focused activities. This improves job satisfaction among teachers and enhances educational outcomes, as teachers have more time and energy to devote to their students. Furthermore, reducing administrative burdens can lower stress levels and job satisfaction, which is crucial for teacher retention and professional well-being.

In conclusion, integrating AI in automating administrative tasks presents a significant opportunity to enhance the efficiency and effectiveness of educational environments. By reducing the burden of routine administrative duties, AI allows educators to focus more on what they do best—teaching, mentoring, and inspiring students. As AI technology continues to evolve, its role in streamlining educational administration promises to empower teachers further and enrich students' learning experiences, heralding a new era of efficiency and focus in education.

2.6 ENHANCING LANGUAGE LEARNING WITH NATURAL LANGUAGE PROCESSING TOOLS

In language education, integrating Artificial Intelligence, particularly through Natural Language Processing (NLP) tools, reshapes how language skills are taught and refined. NLP, a facet of AI that enables computers to understand and interact with human language, offers several transformative benefits for language learners, from personalized practice and feedback to nuanced cultural understanding.

Language Practice and Feedback

One of the most significant advantages of NLP in language learning is its ability to provide students with consistent, personalized practice and immediate feedback. NLP tools are designed to interact with students in the target language, offering exercises that mimic real-life conversations and writing scenarios. These tools can evaluate a student's language use in real-time, from pronunciation to grammar and vocabulary usage, providing instant corrections and suggestions for improvement. This immediate feedback is crucial, allowing learners to correct mistakes and internalize correct usage promptly, accelerating the learning process. Furthermore, because NLP enables personalized interactions, each student can practice at their own pace, focusing on areas that need improvement and enhancing the overall learning efficiency.

Customized Language Learning Experiences

The power of AI to customize learning experiences shines exceptionally bright in language education. NLP technologies can assess learners' proficiency and tailor the learning content accordingly. For example, if a learner struggles with advanced verb conjugations, the NLP system can generate specific exercises to practice those skills, possibly reintroducing basic concepts if necessary. Additionally, these tools can adapt to the student's preferred learning styles—whether they learn better through visual aids, written exercises, or auditory cues—thus making the learning experience much more effective and engaging.

Voice Recognition and Interaction

Voice recognition technology, enhanced by AI and NLP, plays a critical role in language learning by facilitating interactive speaking exercises. These tools enable students to speak directly to the AI, which can then process and understand their input, regardless of accents or dialects. The sophistication of modern AI allows these interactions to be incredibly natural, providing learners with a conversational partner that is always available, patient, and informative. This constant practice can significantly improve pronunciation and fluency, as learners can engage in dialogue without fearing judgment, which can often inhibit practice in more public settings.

Cultural Nuance Understanding

Understanding a language's cultural context is mastering its syntax and vocabulary. Advanced NLP tools can now teach cultural nuances embedded in language, helping learners translate words and grasp their appropriate use in different social contexts. This includes understanding idioms, gestures, and social norms unique to each culture. For instance, an NLP tool might explain why specific phrases are used only in formal situations or why some words can have different meanings based on the context. This deep understanding of cultural nuances is essential for achieving true fluency and using the language effectively and respectfully in real-world interactions.

These applications of AI and NLP in language learning enhance the effectiveness of educational programs and make language learning much more accessible and engaging. By providing personalized, interactive, and culturally informed learning experiences, NLP tools are transforming language education, enabling students to achieve proficiency with unprecedented speed and ease.

As we close this chapter on the practical applications of AI in the classroom, it's evident that integrating AI across different aspects of education offers substantial benefits— from personalized learning paths and enhanced assessments to innovative game-based learning and efficient administrative operations. These tools not only streamline educational processes but also enrich the learning experience for students, making education more engaging, accessible, and effective. Looking ahead, the subsequent chapters will delve deeper into the ethical considerations of AI in education, preparing you to navigate this dynamic landscape with an informed and conscientious approach.

3

NAVIGATING CHALLENGES AND ETHICAL CONSIDERATIONS

As we continue to weave the rich tapestry of AI into the fabric of our educational systems, we encounter a spectrum of challenges that require our attention and conscientious action. One such critical challenge is ensuring the integrity of academic work in an era when AI tools are readily accessible and capable of performing complex tasks. This chapter aims to delve into the nuances of academic honesty in the digital age, equipping you with strategies to design AI-resistant assignments and fostering an environment where integrity is upheld amidst technological advancements.

3.1 DESIGNING AI-RESISTANT ASSIGNMENTS TO COMBAT ACADEMIC DISHONESTY

Understanding AI's Role in Cheating

The advent of sophisticated AI tools has introduced novel ways for students to bypass traditional learning processes, inadvertently fostering opportunities for academic dishonesty. Tools such as advanced text generators and problem solvers can, if misused, enable students to complete assignments without engaging deeply with the material or applying critical thinking. This undermines the learning objectives and poses significant challenges in assessing students' understanding and capabilities. Recognizing this, it becomes imperative to design assignments that not only leverage the benefits of AI but also mitigate its potential misuse.

AI-resistant assignments are necessary to ensure students engage in higher-order thinking—a skill set AI cannot mimic. These skills, which include analysis, evaluation, and creation, are essential for students to develop a deep understanding of the subject matter and to apply knowledge in novel situations. By focusing on these areas, assignments can encourage genuine student engagement and learning, reducing the temptation and effectiveness of taking shortcuts through AI assistance.

Strategies for AI-Resistant Design

Crafting assignments that promote critical thinking and require a personalized understanding of the material involves several strategic approaches. First, consider incorporating project-based learning, where students are tasked with creating unique outputs such as research projects, presentations, or creative works. These tasks require students to draw on multiple information sources, synthesize ideas, and produce a coherent output that reflects a deep engagement with the topic.

Secondly, diversify the types of assessments. Beyond traditional tests and quizzes, include assignments requiring practical skills, group collaborations, and real-world problem-solving demonstrations. These varied forms of assessment can make it more difficult for students to substitute AI's capabilities for their understanding and effort.

Additionally, integrate dynamic and adaptive questioning in your assessments. Tools that randomize question elements or adapt based on the student's responses can be particularly effective. These methods reduce the feasibility of cheating and enhance the assessment's ability to gauge student comprehension across a broader range of topics accurately.

Role of Open-Ended Questions

Open-ended questions are instrumental in cultivating a learning environment that prioritizes critical thinking over rote memorization. By requiring students to elaborate on their answers, analyze scenarios, or propose solutions to complex problems, these questions demand a level of engagement that simple fact recall does not. Open-ended questions also provide insights into students' analytical and creative capabilities, clearly showing their understanding and skills.

Incorporating open-ended questions into assignments encourages students to develop and articulate their thoughts, opinions, and conclusions about the learning material. This makes it difficult for AI to complete the assignments successfully and enhances the educational value of the tasks, promoting deeper learning and retention of the subject matter.

Monitoring and Detection Techniques

It is crucial to employ robust monitoring and detection techniques to ensure that AI tools are used appropriately and detect academic dishonesty. Educational technologies that track how students interact with assignments can provide valuable insights into the authenticity of their work. For example, software that analyzes typing speed, question response times, and resource use can help identify irregularities that may indicate improper use of AI.

Additionally, investing in plagiarism detection software that has been updated to recognize AI-generated content can be an effective measure. These tools compare student submissions against a vast database of known sources and against other student submissions, which can help identify traditional plagiarism and submissions that may have been generated through AI.

By understanding the potential for AI to impact academic integrity, employing strategies to design AI-resistant assignments, and utilizing effective monitoring and detection techniques, you can maintain the rigor and authenticity of scholarly work. This approach not only upholds the standards of your educational institution but also ensures that students reap the full benefits of their educational experiences, equipped with the skills and knowledge they need to succeed in an increasingly complex world.

3.2 ETHICAL CONSIDERATIONS IN AI: BIAS AND FAIRNESS

In education, where equity and fairness form the cornerstone of pedagogical principles, integrating Artificial Intelligence (AI) introduces complex ethical considerations that demand your meticulous attention. Central among these is the issue of bias in AI, a phenomenon that can subtly undermine the equity of educational practices if not adequately addressed. Bias in AI refers to systematic and unfair discrimination often unintentionally embedded within algorithms. This can manifest in academics as skewed decision-making in student assessments, admissions, and resource allocation, potentially disadvantaging certain groups of students and thereby affecting fairness and equality in learning outcomes.

AI bias often stems from the training data used to educate AI systems. When this data lacks representation from diverse student populations or carries historical biases, it can lead AI to replicate or even magnify these biases. For instance, an AI tool evaluating student essays might rely on training data that favors a specific linguistic style, creating a disadvantage for students from varied cultural or socio-economic backgrounds. Additionally, the design of AI algorithms may favor specifics over others based on their initial development priorities. These subtle biases, unless closely examined, can significantly undermine educational equity.

A proactive and multifaceted approach is essential to mitigate the risks of AI bias. Firstly, educators and AI developers must collaborate closely to ensure a deep understanding of where biases might occur and actively seek to eliminate these risks from the outset. This involves meticulously selecting and scrutinizing training data to ensure it is broad, diverse, and inclusive of various student demographics and learning styles. Regular audits of AI algorithms are also crucial; these should be conducted by independent evaluators who can assess the AI's decisions for fairness and accuracy.

Moreover, bias mitigation must be an ongoing commitment. AI systems should not only be designed with fairness in mind but must also be continuously monitored and updated to adapt to new data and evolving educational contexts. This dynamic approach ensures that AI tools remain fair and effective as they learn and develop. Growing feedback mechanisms that allow students and educators to report potential biases in AI decisions can provide real-time data to inform these updates. Additionally, transparency in AI operations should be prioritized, ensuring that all stakeholders understand how AI tools make decisions. This transparency is crucial for building trust and ensuring accountability, as it allows stakeholders to challenge and question AI decisions that seem unfair or incorrect.

This way, the commitment to fairness and equity in using AI in education becomes a shared responsibility among all stakeholders. By fostering an environment of continuous learning, vigilance, and collaboration, you can ensure that AI is a tool for enhancing educational fairness rather than an accidental source of bias. This approach aligns with the ethical standards expected in academics and improves AI's effectiveness and credibility as a transformative educational tool.

3.3 PROTECTING STUDENT PRIVACY WHEN USING AI TOOLS

In the digital age, the sanctity of personal information is paramount, and this holds especially true in education, where sensitive student data is frequently handled. As AI tools become more integrated into educational frameworks, understanding and addressing potential privacy concerns is not merely an option but a necessity. The primary concerns around student data privacy involve the unauthorized access to or misuse of information, which can have far-reaching consequences on a student's academic and personal life. Integrating AI tools in education requires a meticulous approach to managing these risks, ensuring that student data is utilized effectively and protected rigorously.

Central to this protective effort is adherence to regulatory compliance. Laws such as the Family Educational Rights and Privacy Act (FERPA) in the United States and the General Data Protection Regulation (GDPR) in Europe provide frameworks that govern the use of student data. FERPA, for instance, sets out requirements for protecting the privacy of student education records, stipulating conditions under which information may be disclosed without consent. Similarly, GDPR regulates data processing and mandates explicit consent for data collection, ensuring that individuals within the EU have control over their data. Understanding these regulations is crucial for educators and institutions to navigate the legal landscape of data use in education, ensuring that AI tools are implemented in a manner that is both effective and compliant with the law.

Best practices for data protection involve several vital strategies that can significantly enhance the security and integrity of student information. Data anonymization, for example, plays a critical role in safeguarding privacy. This process involves stripping personally identifiable information from student data before it is used for analysis. By doing so, the data can still be utilized to glean insights and improve educational practices without risking the exposure of individual student identities. Additionally, secure data storage solutions are essential. This includes using encrypted databases and secure cloud services to store sensitive information, protecting it from unauthorized access and potential breaches. Regular audits and updates to these storage systems also help maintain a robust defense against evolving external threats.

Educating stakeholders about data use and protection nuances is another cornerstone of effective data management. Students, parents, and educators must know how student data is collected, used, and protected. This involves transparent communication from educational institutions, providing clear and accessible information about data practices. Workshops, seminars, and informational materials can be practical tools in disseminating this knowledge, helping to build a community that is informed and vigilant about data privacy. Moreover, allowing stakeholders to voice their concerns and questions about data practices can foster an environment of trust and cooperation, ensuring that privacy considerations are addressed comprehensively.

By addressing these critical areas—privacy concerns, regulatory compliance, best practices for data protection, and educating stakeholders—educators can navigate the complexities of using AI tools in education responsibly. This ensures compliance with legal standards and builds a foundation of trust and safety essential for the effective use of technology in educational settings. As AI continues to evolve and integrate more deeply into educational practices, maintaining this commitment to student privacy will be crucial in harnessing the full potential of AI tools while upholding the ethical standards that define educational excellence.

3.4 ADDRESSING THE DIGITAL DIVIDE: AI ACCESSIBILITY IN DIVERSE EDUCATIONAL SETTINGS

The 'digital divide' in education refers to the gap between individuals with access to modern information and communication technology and those without limited access. This divide can significantly impact educational programs' effectiveness, particularly when integrating AI into teaching and learning processes. In under-resourced schools, where access to high-speed internet and cutting-edge technology is often limited, the potential benefits of AI in enhancing educational outcomes seem like a distant reality. Addressing this digital divide is crucial for equity in education and ensuring that all students are prepared for a future increasingly dominated by technology.

One effective strategy for bridging this gap involves enhancing infrastructure in technologically underserved communities. This can be achieved through initiatives like securing grants for technology upgrades, which can provide the necessary funds to acquire hardware such as computers and smart devices and to improve internet connectivity. Another approach is the implementation of mobile tech labs, which are buses or vans equipped with high-tech learning facilities. These mobile labs can travel to different schools and communities, providing students and teachers access to AI tools and internet connectivity, temporarily alleviating the limitations of poor infrastructure.

Moreover, developing and deploying low-bandwidth AI applications can be pivotal in making AI accessible in areas with limited internet access. These applications are designed to require minimal data usage, allowing them to be used effectively even with slow internet speeds. For instance, AI-driven educational software can be optimized to run offline, with capabilities to sync data whenever internet access is available. This allows continuous access to AI tools, ensuring the lack of high-speed internet does not hinder learning.

Partnerships between educational institutions and technology companies can further address the digital divide. These collaborations can leverage tech companies' expertise and resources to provide state-of-the-art technological access to under-resourced schools. For example, tech companies can donate AI-powered software or hardware and provide technical support and training for educators. Government agencies and non-profits can also play a crucial role by funding initiatives to enhance technological infrastructure and advocating for policies that support equitable access to technology.

The impact of these initiatives can be profound, as illustrated by several successful case studies. For instance, a rural school district in Africa saw significant improvements in student engagement and learning outcomes after a non-profit organization partnered with a tech company to provide solar-powered computers and satellite internet. The AI software installed on these computers helped personalize learning for students, many of whom were accessing digital learning tools for the first time. In another example, a school in a low-income neighborhood in Brazil used a government grant to install a high-speed broadband connection and train teachers to integrate AI tools into their teaching. The program improved students' computer literacy and enhanced their learning in mathematics and science, where AI tools provided personalized tutoring and feedback.

These examples underscore the importance of addressing the digital divide and ensuring that AI tools are accessible to all students, regardless of their socio-economic or geographical background. By implementing targeted strategies and fostering partnerships, educators and policymakers can work together to close the gap in technology access, paving the way for a more inclusive and equitable educational landscape. This commitment to digital inclusivity is essential for preparing all students to thrive in an increasingly digital world, ensuring they have the skills and knowledge needed to succeed in the 21st century.

3.5 BALANCING AI AND HUMAN INTERACTION IN TEACHING

Integrating Artificial Intelligence (AI) into the educational sphere presents a transformative shift in teaching methodologies. Yet, it raises crucial considerations about the balance between technology and the human touch fundamental to effective teaching. AI should be viewed as a complement to, not a replacement for, the nuanced and irreplaceable elements of human interaction in education. This balance is crucial in preserving the essence of teaching as a profoundly human endeavor that imparts knowledge and critical social and emotional skills.

The complementary role of AI in education centers around its capability to enhance the efficiency and personalization of learning experiences while allowing educators to dedicate more time to direct student engagement. AI excels at processing large datasets, managing routine tasks, and adapting learning paths to meet individual student needs. However, while essential, these tasks only encompass part of the spectrum of teaching. Teaching involves empathy, understanding, motivation, and the ability to inspire—inherently human qualities that algorithms cannot replicate. For instance, while AI can provide feedback on a student's mathematical calculations, it cannot perceive their frustration or offer encouragement and nuanced explanations that might break through their specific learning barriers.

To integrate AI tools effectively while maintaining meaningful personal interactions, educators should focus on strategies that leverage AI for administrative and analytical tasks while prioritizing human interaction for mentoring, discussion, and support activities. For example, AI can track student progress and highlight areas where individual students may need additional support, allowing the teacher to focus more on providing targeted interventions rather than spending extensive time on data analysis. Additionally, AI-driven platforms can handle the initial stages of content delivery through tailored instructional videos and adaptive quizzes, freeing up classroom time for interactive discussions, group projects, and one-on-one sessions that foster more profound understanding and connection.

AI is also a powerful support tool in managing educators' expansive and often overwhelming administrative responsibilities. Automating attendance, grading standard assignments, and scheduling can significantly reduce teachers' workloads, enabling them to allocate more energy and time toward engaging with students on a personal and impactful level. This shift enhances the quality of education and contributes to teacher satisfaction and well-being, which is crucial for long-term educational success.

Moreover, focusing on emotional and social learning is imperative, as these elements are critical to student development and best facilitated through human interaction. While AI can assist in delivering educational content and personalizing learning pathways, it cannot teach social skills, empathy, and emotional resilience. Activities that require collaboration, negotiation, and real-time interpersonal skills should be structured to emphasize human interaction without AI interference. Educators can create environments encouraging students to collaborate on projects, discuss diverse viewpoints, and engage in community service activities, thereby developing their social and emotional competencies.

Integrating AI into education should enhance human interaction rather than diminish it. By strategically deploying AI in the most effective areas and maintaining a strong focus on the human aspects of teaching, educators can create a harmonious blend of technology and personal engagement that prepares students for a future where emotional intelligence and technological proficiency are equally valued. This balanced approach ensures that as we leverage the advancements in AI, we continue to cherish and cultivate the irreplaceable human connections at the heart of education.

3.6 LEGAL IMPLICATIONS OF AI IN THE CLASSROOM

Integrating Artificial Intelligence (AI) into educational environments while opening avenues for enhanced learning and operational efficiency also navigates a complex landscape of legal considerations. As educators and institutions embrace this technology, it is imperative to understand the legal frameworks that govern its use and the potential liabilities that may arise. Key concerns include liability issues related to the use of AI in education and intellectual property rights concerning AI-generated content and student-created materials.

Overview of Legal Concerns

AI's role in the classroom extends beyond a pedagogical tool; it also introduces potential legal implications that educational institutions must carefully manage. Liability concerns, for instance, can arise from the misuse of AI technologies or failures in AI systems that lead to inaccuracies in student assessments or data breaches. Intellectual property rights are another significant area of legal concern, particularly regarding the ownership of AI-generated content and the use of such content within educational settings. As AI continues to evolve, staying ahead of these legal issues is crucial for ensuring its integration into educational practices is practical and compliant with existing laws.

Navigating Liability Issues

Liability issues in the context of AI in education primarily revolve around the potential for harm from using these technologies. For example, if an AI-driven platform mistakenly fails a student due to an error in its programming, the institution could face legal repercussions from the affected parties. Similarly, if an AI system that manages student data is compromised, leading to a data breach, the institution could be liable for failing to protect sensitive information.

Educational institutions must implement robust risk management strategies to mitigate these risks. This includes conducting thorough assessments of AI technologies before integrating them into the academic environment, ensuring they meet all applicable safety and privacy standards. Regular audits and updates to AI systems can also help prevent errors and security vulnerabilities that could lead to liability issues. Furthermore, clear and comprehensive contracts with AI vendors should outline responsibility for failures or breaches, ensuring that institutions are legally protected in such events.

Intellectual Property in AI

The rise of AI has also stirred significant discussions around intellectual property rights, particularly concerning content generated by AI tools and materials created by students using AI technologies. The main question revolves around who owns the rights to AI-generated works. Is it the developer of the AI, the user who interacted with the AI, or the institution that owns the AI software? These questions are not merely academic; they have practical implications for how materials are used, shared, and monetized within educational settings.

Educational institutions must navigate these intellectual property challenges by developing clear policies and agreements that specify ownership and usage rights for AI-generated content. This might involve negotiating terms with AI vendors to ensure that the institution retains ownership of the content created by their students using AI tools. Additionally, understanding and adhering to copyright laws that pertain to digital content and software is crucial in preventing infringement disputes and ensuring that the educational use of AI remains within legal boundaries.

Staying Informed on Legal Changes

The legal landscape regarding AI in education continually evolves, with new laws and regulations being proposed and implemented as the technology progresses. For educators and institutions, staying informed about these legal developments is critical. This ensures compliance with current laws and prepares educational entities to adapt to incoming changes that might affect how AI tools are used in classrooms.

Regular training sessions for educators and administrative staff on the latest legal developments related to AI can help maintain a knowledgeable and compliant educational environment. Subscriptions to legal updates, attending relevant workshops and seminars, and consulting with legal experts in educational technology are all proactive measures institutions can take to stay informed and ahead of legal issues in AI.

By addressing these legal implications of AI in the classroom —from liability concerns to intellectual property issues— educational institutions can better navigate the complexities of integrating AI into their teaching and administrative practices. This not only protects the institutions legally but also ensures that the benefits of AI are harnessed in a manner that is ethical, responsible, and compliant with the law.

4

AI TOOLS AND TECHNOLOGIES FOR TODAY'S EDUCATOR

As we continue to navigate the ever-evolving landscape of educational technology, integrating Artificial Intelligence (AI) into our classrooms isn't just an innovation; it becomes a pivotal strategy in enhancing teaching efficacy and student learning outcomes. This chapter delves deeply into the versatile arsenal of available AI tools, which can significantly transform educational environments. These tools are not merely technological advancements; they are partners in education designed to streamline processes, enhance learning, and ensure that no student is left behind due to accessibility issues.

4.1 AI TOOLS AND THEIR FUNCTIONALITIES IN EDUCATION

In the dynamic world of educational technology, various AI tools have emerged, each offering unique functionalities that cater to different aspects of the educational process. From administrative automation tools that help manage day-today tasks to sophisticated interactive learning platforms, AI is reshaping the academic landscape.

One notable example is AI-driven Learning Management Systems (LMS) like Canvas and Moodle. These platforms utilize AI to provide personalized learning experiences and predictive analytics that help educators identify students needing additional support. They automate administrative tasks such as grading and feedback, allowing educators to focus more on teaching rather than tedious tasks. Furthermore, AI in LMS can dynamically adapt course content based on student performance, ensuring that each student receives a tailored learning experience that maximizes their understanding and retention of course materials.

Another transformative tool is AI tutoring systems, such as Carnegie Learning's MATHia. Using sophisticated algorithms, these platforms offer students step-by-step guidance through complex problems, adapting to the student's needs in real-time. This personalized approach enhances learning and allows the system to identify and address individual learning gaps, contributing significantly to the student's overall success in the subject.

Moreover, AI-powered educational games like those developed by the age of Learning integrate immersive, interactive learning with rigorous academic content to engage students in a compelling narrative. These tools make learning enjoyable and engaging, encouraging students to delve deeper into subjects and explore concepts they might find challenging in a traditional educational setting.

Accessibility and Integration of AI Tools in Education

The impact of AI tools extends beyond their functionalities; their integration into educational systems plays a crucial role in their effectiveness. A significant advantage of modern AI educational tools is their emphasis on accessibility and usability. Developers have prioritized making these tools intuitive and easy to navigate, ensuring educators and students can use them without extensive technological expertise. Furthermore, many AI tools now incorporate accessibility features to accommodate users with disabilities, such as text-to-speech functions, screen readers, and customizable interfaces. These features ensure that all students have equal access to educational technologies regardless of their physical abilities.

The integration of AI tools into existing educational infrastructures is also streamlined. Most modern AI tools are designed to be compatible with existing LMS and other academic software, facilitating a seamless transition and integration. For instance, AI analytics tools can often be plugged into existing LMS to offer deeper insights into student performance without disrupting the workflow.

Implementing these AI tools into their teaching toolkit with the right strategies can be straightforward for educators. It often begins with identifying the specific needs of their classroom and selecting AI tools that align with these requirements. Training and professional development sessions can be beneficial in familiarizing educators with these tools, empowering them to use AI not just as a supplementary resource but as an integral part of their teaching strategy.

As AI advances, its role in education becomes increasingly significant. It offers tools and technologies that promise to enhance the teaching and learning experience. These AI solutions not only automate administrative tasks and personalize learning but also open up new possibilities for accessibility, ensuring that every student has the opportunity to succeed. Integrating these tools into our educational practices enhances our teaching capabilities and inspires our students to reach their full potential in an increasingly digital world.

4.2 EVALUATING AI CONTENT CREATORS FOR CLASSROOM USE

In the vast educational technology ecosystem, AI content creators stand out as pivotal tools capable of revolutionizing the delivery of academic content. As educators, your discernment in selecting and implementing these AI tools is crucial. The criteria for evaluating AI content creators should emphasize accuracy of content, alignment with educational standards, and adaptability to diverse learning styles. Accuracy is fundamental because educational content directly influences learning outcomes; hence, AI-generated materials must be precise and reliable. Alignment with educational standards ensures that the content supports and enhances the curriculum, reinforcing what is taught through traditional methods. Lastly, adaptability to learning styles is vital for addressing how students perceive and assimilate information, ensuring all students can benefit from the technology.

Let's consider the implementation of an AI content creator like Quillionz, which uses AI to generate quiz questions and learning summaries based on the content provided. In a classroom setting, an educator can input sections of a textbook or notes from a lesson, and Quillionz creates customized quizzes that test students on the critical points of the lesson. This tool has been particularly effective in reinforcing learning, allowing students to engage with the material actively and providing educators with insights into areas where students might struggle. The adaptability of Quillionz to generate content based on different subjects and complexity levels exemplifies the importance of flexible AI tools in education.

However, while the benefits are significant, there are potential pitfalls in using AI content creators that you must be wary of. One common challenge is the issue of data biases. AI systems learn from large datasets; if these datasets are diverse and inclusive, the AI's output can be biased. This might result in content that needs to adequately reflect multicultural perspectives or favor one demographic over another, potentially leading to skewed perceptions and educational experiences. Another challenge is the over-reliance on automated content, which might discourage deeper engagement with the material if students or educators view AI-generated content as a complete substitute for traditional learning methods.

Addressing these challenges involves a combination of awareness, proactive strategy, and continuous oversight. Educators should be vigilant about examining AI-generated content for potential biases by involving diverse groups of students and colleagues in reviewing materials. Additionally,

AI content should complement traditional teaching methods, not replace them. This ensures a balanced approach to education, where AI tools enhance the learning experience rather than diminish the educator's role.

Best practices for incorporating AI content creators into teaching start with a clear strategy that defines what these tools are intended to achieve. For instance, AI-generated quizzes can be used as supplementary tools for revision and testing, while AI-generated summaries can help students with learning disabilities grasp vital concepts more clearly. Educators should also ensure regular updates and feedback loops with the AI tool providers to keep the software aligned with the latest educational standards and learning sciences. Training sessions for educators and student feedback mechanisms can ensure that AI content creators are optimized, enhancing teaching efficacy and student engagement.

In deploying AI content creators, the focus should always remain on enhancing educational outcomes and fostering an inclusive, adaptive learning environment. By carefully selecting, implementing, and monitoring AI tools, educators can significantly enrich the learning experience, ensuring that students are well-prepared for their exams and a world where technology and learning go hand in hand.

4.3 THE BEST AI PLATFORMS FOR STEM EDUCATION

In the specialized realm of STEM (Science, Technology, Engineering, and Mathematics) education, specific AI platforms stand out for their tailored functionalities that significantly enhance both teaching and learning experiences.

These platforms are tools and transformative environments that reshape how STEM subjects are taught and understood. Let's explore some of the top AI platforms that have been making notable impacts in STEM classrooms.

One exemplary platform is Wolfram Alpha, an AI-driven computational knowledge engine that excels in solving complex mathematical problems and providing step-by-step solutions. This tool is invaluable for mathematics and engineering education, offering students and educators a powerful resource for exploring and understanding complicated equations and computational thinking. Its capability to generate interactive visuals for mathematical concepts helps demystify abstract theories and engage students more profoundly.

Another innovative platform is Labster, which provides virtual laboratory simulations. This tool allows students to conduct scientific experiments in an online environment that replicates physical labs. Labster's simulations cover a range of scientific disciplines, including biology, chemistry, and physics, making it a versatile tool for schools that may lack extensive laboratory facilities. Each simulation integrates theoretical knowledge and practical experimentation, enhancing students' understanding and retention of scientific concepts.

Integrating IBM's Watson into the education sector has also proven beneficial, particularly in the context of personalized learning. Watson's AI excels at adapting learning paths based on individual student responses. In STEM education, where understanding foundational concepts is crucial, Watson's ability to personalize content and pace according to each student's learning needs results in more effective education outcomes.

Enhancing Experimentation and Discovery

These AI platforms do more than just provide information; they create opportunities for experimentation and discovery, which are core to STEM learning. Virtual labs, such as those offered by Labster, allow students to perform experiments that would be too costly, dangerous, or impossible to conduct in a school setting. These virtual environments encourage students to make hypotheses, conduct experiments, and learn from their failures in a risk-free setting, fostering a hands-on approach to learning that is both safe and cost-effective.

Moreover, platforms like Wolfram Alpha encourage exploration through interactive elements that allow students to manipulate variables and instantly see the effects. This real-time interaction with mathematical and scientific models provides a deeper understanding of the underlying principles and enhances critical thinking skills. The immediate feedback available through these platforms allows students to learn through discovery, exploring concepts at their own pace and according to their interest levels, which is often not feasible in a traditional classroom setting.

Real-World Application

AI in STEM education bridges the gap between theoretical knowledge and real-world application. Using platforms like Autodesk Tinkercad, students learn to design, model, and test objects and systems in a virtual environment that mirrors real-world engineering tasks. Tinkercad, for example, allows students to create 3D designs and simulations that can be used in actual 3D printing projects, directly linking classroom activities with real-world applications.

These applications extend beyond the classroom. For instance, AI-powered data analysis tools can process complex data sets from real-world scenarios, such as weather patterns or traffic flows, allowing students to apply mathematical and computational concepts to solve practical problems. This enhances learning outcomes and prepares students for future careers in STEM fields, where the ability to apply classroom knowledge in practical settings is invaluable.

Collaboration Features

Collaboration is another significant aspect of STEM education that is greatly enhanced by AI platforms. Tools like Microsoft Teams for Education integrate seamlessly with AI functionalities to facilitate group projects and collaborative research. These platforms provide a shared space where students can work together synchronously despite physical distances. AI-driven recommendations can suggest resources, divide tasks based on individual strengths, and even assess group interactions to optimize collaborative efforts.

Furthermore, AI platforms can facilitate a new level of interaction between students and teachers. Through AI-driven analytics, educators can gain insights into each student's progress and challenges, allowing them to provide targeted support. This fosters a more interactive learning environment where teachers guide students through personalized learning journeys, closely monitoring their progress and adapting instructions to meet each student's unique needs.

In summary, integrating AI in STEM education through these platforms enhances education delivery and transforms it into a more interactive, engaging, and practical experience. By leveraging AI tools, STEM education can transcend traditional barriers, offering students a more profound, practical, and collaborative approach to learning that prepares them for future challenges.

4.4 AI IN ARTS AND HUMANITIES: EXPANDING CREATIVE BOUNDARIES

Integrating AI into the arts and humanities marks a fascinating evolution in the rich tapestry of learning. Technology not only supports but actively enhances creativity and interdisciplinary understanding. AI, often perceived as a tool for analytical fields, is instrumental in music, visual arts, and literature, fostering new forms of creative expression and cultural exploration. These applications demonstrate AI's versatility and its potential to enrich human creativity.

In the realm of music, AI systems like AIVA (Artificial Intelligence Virtual Artist) are composing symphonies by learning from a vast database of classical music. AIVA analyzes patterns in compositions by great masters such as Bach and Beethoven and uses this knowledge to generate original pieces that are both dynamic and structurally sound. This illustrates an extraordinary leap where AI collaborates with musicians, offering tools that extend their creative capabilities and introduce new possibilities for innovation in music composition. Similarly, in visual arts, programs like DeepArt use convolutional neural networks to transform photographs into artworks in the styles of famous painters like Van Gogh and Picasso. This democratizes artistic creation, allowing individuals without formal training to produce art, and deepens our understanding of style and technique in art history.

The integration of AI in literature is equally transformative. Tools like GPT-3, a language prediction model, assist authors by generating narrative suggestions, dialogues, and even poetic compositions. Such tools can serve as a collaborative partner for writers, providing inspiration and new perspectives that enrich the storytelling process. These AI applications do not replace the artist but rather enhance their creative process, pushing the boundaries of traditional artistic expression and opening up new avenues for innovation and exploration.

The potential of AI tools to bridge the gap between the arts and more technical subjects is particularly noteworthy. This interdisciplinary approach enhances learning and fosters a holistic educational environment where students can see and understand the connections between different fields of study. For instance, AI applications that analyze music can teach mathematical concepts such as patterns and probabilities, while AI-driven analysis of art styles can incorporate elements of geometry and physics. This convergence encourages students to develop a multifaceted understanding of subjects, promoting cognitive flexibility and a deeper appreciation for the arts and the sciences.

Incorporating Cultural Context in AI Applications

Incorporating cultural context in AI applications within the arts and humanities is crucial for ensuring that these tools support and celebrate diversity. AI systems that analyze and generate artistic content must be trained on diverse datasets that reflect various cultural expressions and perspectives. This prevents the homogenization of creative outputs and ensures that AI tools are sensitive to cultural nuances and can be used to promote intercultural understanding and appreciation.

For example, AI used in analyzing historical data can be programmed to recognize and respect cultural context, providing insights informed by understanding the specific social, historical, and cultural dynamics. Such an approach enriches the analysis and educates users about the importance of context in interpreting historical and cultural information. Similarly, AI-driven language learning tools that adapt to include idiomatic expressions, regional dialects, and cultural references can offer a more nuanced and comprehensive language learning experience that respects and celebrates linguistic diversity.

Enhancing Critical Thinking and Analysis

AI's role in enhancing critical thinking and analytical skills in the arts and humanities education is particularly significant. AI-driven tools can analyze vast amounts of text, music, or art, identifying patterns, themes, and historical influences that might not be immediately apparent. This can be an invaluable resource for students and scholars, providing new insights and perspectives that deepen their understanding of a subject.

For instance, AI can perform stylistic analysis of literature, helping students identify an author's unique voice, themes, and the evolution of their writing style over time. In art history, AI tools can analyze visual elements across thousands of artworks to track influences and trends, providing students with a macro-view of artistic movements that complements traditional study methods. AI's analytical capabilities support academic research and enhance pedagogical strategies, making learning more engaging and insightful.

AI significantly contributes to the arts and humanities through these creative and interdisciplinary applications, challenging the notion that technology is solely a scientific tool. By fostering creativity, enhancing interdisciplinary learning, respecting cultural contexts, and supporting analytical thinking, AI becomes a pivotal element in modern education, offering students and educators a richer, more diverse educational experience. As we continue to explore and integrate these tools, the potential for discoveries and innovations in arts and humanities education is boundless, promising an exciting future where technology and creativity converge to expand the horizons of what is possible in learning and expression.

4.5 CLOUD-BASED AI TOOLS: ENHANCING COLLABORATION AND ACCESSIBILITY

In the evolving educational technology landscape, cloud-based AI tools represent a significant advancement, offering robust solutions that cater to the dynamic needs of modern educational environments. These tools operate on cloud computing platforms, meaning they utilize remote servers for processing and data storage rather than local servers or personal computers. This setup provides several distinct advantages, particularly scalability, remote accessibility, and cost-effectiveness. Cloud-based AI tools can quickly scale to accommodate an increasing number of users or a sudden surge in data usage, making them ideal for educational institutions that experience variable demands. Furthermore, these tools are accessible from any device with internet connectivity, enabling learning and administrative activities to continue seamlessly outside of traditional classroom settings—a feature that has become particularly crucial in the wake of increasing remote learning initiatives.

The scalability of cloud-based AI tools allows educational institutions to simultaneously provide personalized learning experiences to many students. For example, AI-driven adaptive learning platforms hosted on the cloud can manage thousands of individual learner profiles, adapting the curriculum in real-time based on each student's progress and needs. This capability not only enhances the learning experience for students by providing them with content tailored to their learning pace and style but also enables educators to monitor and manage these personalized learning paths efficiently.

Remote accessibility is another cornerstone of cloud-based AI tools. It ensures that students and educators can access educational resources, submit assignments, and even participate in interactive learning modules from anywhere, at any time. This level of accessibility is transforming education into a more flexible and inclusive endeavor, accommodating diverse learning schedules and situations. For instance, students who may be unable to attend school due to health issues or geographical constraints can continue their education without disruption, promoting inclusivity and continuity in learning.

Cost-effectiveness also stands out as a significant benefit of cloud-based AI tools. By utilizing cloud infrastructure, educational institutions can save on installing and maintaining physical servers. Cloud providers typically offer flexible payment models based on usage, allowing schools to pay only for the resources they use. Additionally, the cloud service provider handles the maintenance and security of the data, reducing the burden on school IT departments and allowing them to allocate resources to other critical areas.

Examples of Effective Cloud-Based AI Tools in Education

Several cloud-based AI tools have substantially impacted how education is delivered and managed. Google Classroom, for example, utilizes AI and cloud computing to streamline assignment distribution, grading, and feedback. This tool allows teachers to organize courses, provide resources, and interact with students on a platform, significantly improving communication and organization in the educational process. Similarly, the AI component of Google Classroom can analyze submission patterns to help educators identify students needing additional help, enabling timely and targeted intervention.

Another influential tool is AWS Educate, provided by Amazon Web Services, which offers cloud-based learning resources and labs for students and educators. This platform gives users access to real-world cloud technology and AI applications, facilitating practical learning experiences directly applicable to technology and innovation careers. AWS Educate also includes collaboration features that allow students to work on projects in a virtual environment, mirroring the collaborative nature of modern workplaces.

Security Considerations for Cloud-Based AI Tools

While cloud-based AI tools offer numerous benefits, they also raise important security considerations, particularly regarding data protection and privacy. As educational institutions handle a significant amount of sensitive information, ensuring the security of this data within cloud environments is paramount. To mitigate risks, these institutions must choose reputable cloud service providers that comply with stringent security standards and regulations. Data encryption, both in transit and at rest, is a fundamental security measure, ensuring that data is protected from unauthorized access. Additionally, robust authentication and access control mechanisms can prevent unauthorized access to sensitive information.

Regular security assessments and updates are also vital in maintaining the integrity of cloud-based systems. Educational institutions should work closely with cloud providers to ensure that security protocols are regularly reviewed and updated in response to emerging threats. Moreover, educating all users about basic cybersecurity practices, such as recognizing phishing attempts and securing login credentials, can further enhance the security of cloud-based educational tools.

Implementation Strategies for Cloud-Based AI Tools in Educational Settings

Successfully implementing cloud-based AI tools in educational settings requires a strategic approach encompassing technical, pedagogical, and organizational aspects. Initially, assessing the institution's specific needs and selecting tools that align with these needs and the overall educational goals is crucial. Training educators and administrative staff to use these tools effectively is also essential, ensuring they are comfortable and proficient with the technology.

Moreover, integrating cloud-based AI tools should accompany a review and possible adaptation of the curriculum and teaching practices. This ensures that the tools are used as add-ons and integral components of the educational process, enhancing and transforming learning experiences. Continuous monitoring and evaluation of the implementation can provide insights into how effectively the tools are being used and what improvements can be made.

By carefully planning and executing the integration of cloud-based AI tools, educational institutions can enhance the accessibility, efficiency, and quality of education. These tools provide significant operational benefits and support innovative teaching and learning methods that prepare students for a future where technology and education are increasingly intertwined.

4.6 MONITORING LEARNING PROGRESS WITH AI ANALYTICS

In the contemporary educational landscape, AI analytics is a pivotal technology, revolutionizing how educators monitor and enhance student learning. AI analytics provides real-time insights into student performance and engagement by meticulously analyzing data collected during educational activities. This continuous stream of data allows for an unprecedented level of personalization in education, enabling educators to tailor their approaches to meet the unique needs of each student.

AI analytics systems function by gathering vast amounts of data from various student interactions, whether they are answers to quizzes, participation in interactive modules, or responses within educational games. These systems analyze the data to identify patterns and trends that can give educators a deep understanding of how students perform and engage with the material. This might include which concepts students grasp quickly, where they struggle, or how different teaching methods affect their learning. By converting these insights into actionable information, AI analytics allows educators to adjust their teaching strategies in real-time, ensuring they effectively meet their students' learning needs.

Additionally, AI analytics is crucial in identifying students needing additional support. By pinpointing specific areas where a student is struggling, AI systems can alert educators to these issues early, allowing for timely interventions that can make a significant difference in a student's educational journey. For example, suppose a student consistently needs to improve on quizzes involving a particular concept. In that case, the AI system can flag this trend, prompting the educator to provide additional resources or one-on-one support to help the student overcome these challenges.

Data-Driven Decision Making

Integrating AI analytics into educational practices supports a data-driven approach to decision-making. With comprehensive analytics, educators can make informed decisions about curriculum adjustments and teaching strategies. This data-driven approach ensures that decisions are based not on intuition alone but on concrete evidence of what works best to enhance student learning.

For instance, if AI analytics reveal that students achieve better outcomes through visual learning rather than traditional lectures, educators might incorporate more multimedia presentations or interactive simulations into their curriculum. Similarly, suppose the data shows that students engage more deeply with material presented in a gamified format. In that case, this might encourage the adoption of more game-based learning initiatives within the classroom. These adjustments, informed by solid data, can significantly improve educational effectiveness and student satisfaction.

Ethical Considerations in Using AI Analytics

While the benefits of AI analytics in education are substantial, they also bring to light critical ethical considerations that must be navigated carefully. Chief among these is the need to ensure the confidentiality and integrity of student data. Educators and institutions must implement stringent data protection measures to prevent unauthorized access to or manipulation of sensitive information. This involves technical solutions, such as secure data storage and encryption, and comprehensive policies governing data access and usage.

Furthermore, AI analytics must be used wisely. While these systems can provide valuable insights, they should not be used to label or limit students based on their performance data. Care must be taken to ensure that AI analytics serve as a tool for empowerment rather than discrimination, supporting all students in reaching their full potential regardless of their background or abilities.

By addressing these ethical considerations and using AI analytics responsibly, educators can harness the power of data to transform educational outcomes. AI analytics offers a window into the learning process that was previously unavailable, providing educators with the tools they need to tailor their teaching to the needs of their students and make informed decisions that enhance educational quality. This technology does not replace the human touch in education but rather augments it, offering a blend of personalization and efficiency that can bring out the best in both teachers and students.

As we continue to explore the capabilities of AI in education, it becomes evident that these technologies offer not just incremental improvements but a transformation of the educational landscape. The insights provided by AI analytics, the personalization afforded by adaptive learning systems, and the efficiencies introduced through administrative automation all contribute to a more effective, engaging, and inclusive educational environment. Looking ahead, the potential of AI to further enhance education is vast, promising a future where all students can achieve their full potential with the support of intelligent, responsive educational tools.

5

IMPLEMENTING AI FOR PERSONALIZED AND ADAPTIVE LEARNING

Imagine a classroom where every lesson feels as if crafted just for you, where the pace, content, and teaching style are all perfectly aligned with your individual learning needs. This is not a far-off dream but a tangible reality forged today through AI-driven personalized learning frameworks. As educators and developers, we stand on the brink of a transformative shift in how educational experiences are designed and delivered, leveraging AI to create learning environments that adapt dynamically to each student.

5.1 BUILDING AI-DRIVEN PERSONALIZED LEARNING FRAMEWORKS

Design Principles

The principles of adaptability, scalability, and student-centric design are at the core of any practical AI-driven personalized learning framework. These principles ensure the frameworks are flexible but evolve according to changing educational landscapes and diverse student needs. Adaptability in AI-driven systems means the algorithms can adjust learning paths in real-time based on immediate feedback from student interactions. This fluidity ensures the learning process remains relevant and responsive to each student's pace and progress.

Scalability is equally crucial. Educational tools must be able to expand and accommodate varying numbers of students while maintaining effectiveness. AI's scalability lies in its ability to simultaneously manage extensive datasets from numerous students, applying insights gained across different contexts to benefit individual learning paths. Lastly, a student-centric design insists that these technologies are molded around the student's needs rather than forcing students to adapt to the technology. This approach enhances learning outcomes and ensures that the technology is a supportive tool, enhancing the educational process rather than overshadowing it.

Integration with Curriculum

Integrating AI-driven personalized learning frameworks within existing curriculums requires a delicate balance. These frameworks must complement rather than replace traditional teaching methods. They should act as enablers that enhance the effectiveness of conventional educational approaches. For instance, AI can diagnose a student's existing knowledge of a subject, allowing educators to tailor lessons that fill gaps in understanding while challenging the student with new concepts. This integration fosters a blended learning environment where digital and human resources work together to provide a richer, more effective educational experience.

Integrating AI into the curriculum can be as straightforward as incorporating AI-driven assessments that help educators track progress in real-time or as complex as using AI systems to create individualized learning plans for each student. The key is ensuring that these integrations are seamless and genuinely add value to the educational process rather than complicating or detracting from it.

Use of Learner Data

The power of AI in education largely stems from its ability to continuously utilize data from learner interactions to refine and personalize the learning experience. Every student's click, answer, and interaction with the system feeds into the AI, which uses this data to adjust its educational content. This responsive approach ensures that the learning material remains challenging yet accessible, pushing the student towards higher levels of achievement.

Data privacy and ethical use of information are paramount in this process. Stringent measures must be in place to protect student data and ensure that it is used responsibly. Educators must be transparent with students and guardians about how data is used to enhance learning, build trust, and provide the ethical deployment of AI technologies.

Case Examples

An illustrative example of a successful AI-driven personalized learning implementation can be seen in a high school where AI was used to tailor English language lessons for non-native speakers. The AI system analyzed each student's reading levels and comprehension skills, then adjusted the complexity of the text and the vocabulary exercises according to individual proficiency. This personalized approach helped students improve their language skills more rapidly and effectively than traditional one-size-fits-all methods.

Another example comes from a university where AI-driven frameworks were integrated into a calculus course. The system tracked each student's problem-solving methods, providing personalized hints and tips to guide students through complex equations based on their unique learning styles and previous responses. The result was a notable increase in pass rates and student satisfaction, demonstrating the effectiveness of AI in enhancing understanding and engagement in challenging subjects.

These examples underscore the transformative potential of AI in education, illustrating how technology can be used to craft learning experiences that are not only personalized but profoundly effective. As we continue to explore and implement these AI-driven frameworks, we are not just enhancing educational outcomes but redefining what is possible in teaching and learning, creating a future where every student has the tools and support they need to succeed.

5.2 ADAPTIVE LEARNING SYSTEMS: THEORY TO PRACTICE

Theoretical Background

Adaptive learning systems, rooted in educational theories such as constructivism and cognitive load theory, offer a refined approach to personalized education that adjusts to the learning needs of each student. Constructivism, a theory developed by Jean Piaget and later extended by Lev Vygotsky, posits that learners construct knowledge through experiences and interactions with the world around them. This theory supports the idea that learning best occurs when content is actively constructed rather than passively consumed. Cognitive load theory, introduced by John Sweller, complements this by emphasizing the importance of managing the amount of information processed by the learner's working memory. Too much information can overwhelm the learner, while too little can hinder learning. Adaptive learning systems integrate these theories to create dynamic educational experiences that adjust content complexity and learning paths in real-time based on the learner's cognitive load and individual learning progress.

These systems use sophisticated algorithms to assess each student's interaction with the material, adjusting the complexity and delivery of content to optimize the learning experience. For example, if a student excels in a particular topic, the system can introduce more advanced materials or explore related subjects, thereby maintaining an appropriate challenge level. Conversely, if a student struggles with a concept, the system can simplify the information or provide additional resources and practice opportunities to consolidate understanding before moving forward.

System Components

The architecture of adaptive learning systems typically involves several key components: learner models, content models, and pedagogical models. Learner models track and analyze individual student data to create a dynamic profile of each student's knowledge, skills, and learning preferences. This model is continuously updated as the student interacts with the system, providing a real-time representation of the student's learning journey.

Content models organize the educational material within the system. This includes mapping the curriculum to allow flexibility and adaptation based on the learner's progress. The content is often broken down into smaller, manageable segments that can be rearranged and presented in customized sequences to suit individual learning paths.

Pedagogical models define the instructional strategies employed by the system to deliver content. These models use insights from educational psychology to determine the most effective ways to present information, assess understanding, and provide feedback. They are crucial in ensuring that the system adopts its teaching methods to the needs of each student, aligning with best pedagogical practices.

Practical Implementation

Implementing adaptive classroom learning systems requires careful planning and considering technological and instructional components. Selecting the right technology is foundational. It involves choosing a system that fits the institution's educational goals and is compatible with existing technological infrastructure. This might mean selecting a cloud-based platform that can easily integrate with the school's existing learning management systems and databases.

Training educators on how to use these systems effectively is equally important. Professional development should cover the software's technical aspects and include pedagogical training to help teachers understand how to incorporate adaptive learning into their traditional teaching methods. This might involve workshops or ongoing training sessions where teachers can learn how to interpret the data generated by the system, use it to inform their teaching strategies, and provide appropriate interventions when necessary.

Evaluation and Adjustment

Continuous evaluation is critical to ensuring that adaptive learning systems effectively enhance education. This involves regular assessments of student performance and the system's impact on learning outcomes. The system's data analytics can offer valuable insights into engagement levels, mastery of content, and the effectiveness of different pedagogical approaches. This information can be used to make informed adjustments to the content and the teaching methods.

Moreover, soliciting feedback from students and teachers can provide additional perspectives on the system's effectiveness and areas for improvement. This feedback can be instrumental in refining the adaptive learning system to meet all users' needs better. Adjustments may include updating the content model to include more diverse materials, changing the learner model to track progress better, or incorporating more effective teaching strategies into the pedagogical model.

By understanding the theoretical underpinnings of adaptive learning, carefully assembling the system components, thoughtfully implementing these systems in educational settings, and continuously evaluating and refining the approach, educators can maximize the potential of adaptive learning systems. These systems significantly advance personalized education, offering tailored learning experiences to meet student's diverse needs and help them achieve their full academic potential.

5.3 USING AI TO IDENTIFY AND SUPPORT DIVERSE LEARNING STYLES

Understanding and addressing individual learning styles is critical in crafting educational experiences that maximize student engagement and comprehension. AI, with its capacity to analyze vast amounts of data and identify patterns, is uniquely positioned to transform how educators tailor educational content to meet the varied needs of their students. By examining students' interactions with digital learning materials—how they navigate lessons, the pace at which they learn, their quiz responses, and more—AI can discern whether a student is a visual, auditory, reading/writing, or kinesthetic learner. This identification process is crucial, as it allows educators to understand the preferred learning modalities of each student, paving the way for more personalized and effective teaching strategies.

Once individual learning styles are identified, AI can be instrumental in customizing the delivery of educational content to align with these styles, thereby enhancing learning efficiency and student satisfaction. For visual learners, AI can increase the incorporation of diagrams, videos, and infographics into the learning material, making complex information more accessible and engaging. On the other hand, Auditory learners might benefit from AI-curated podcasts or explanations that they can listen to, which helps reinforce their understanding of the subject matter. For those who prefer reading/writing, AI can provide extensive textual content with interactive notes. At the same time, kinesthetic learners can be engaged through AI-driven simulations or interactive activities that allow learning by doing.

This tailored content delivery bolsters engagement and ensures that each student can grasp and retain complex concepts, catering to their individual learning preferences. Educators can create a more dynamic and responsive learning environment by leveraging AI to adapt how educational content is presented. This environment recognizes and celebrates the diverse ways students absorb and process information, fostering a more inclusive and equitable educational landscape.

Moreover, AI's role extends beyond the initial identification and customization of learning experiences. It also provides critical feedback mechanisms that offer ongoing insights into the effectiveness of tailored content delivery. AI systems can track how students interact with customized content and assess their performance through adaptive assessments, providing educators with real-time feedback on what is working and what isn't. This feedback is invaluable, as it allows educators to continually refine their teaching approaches, ensuring they always align with the students' evolving educational needs.

For example, suppose AI data shows that a group of visual learners is consistently underperforming on assessments despite the use of video content. In that case, the educator might investigate whether the videos are too complex or detailed. They might also consider integrating complementary teaching materials, such as diagrams or interactive visualizations, to provide a richer learning experience. This iterative process, driven by AI, ensures that educational content is tailored to individual learning styles and continuously optimized to meet students' needs effectively.

Implementing AI-driven strategies to support diverse learning styles gives educators a powerful tool that enhances students' learning experience and contributes to a more nuanced understanding of educational diversity. This approach acknowledges each student's unique abilities and preferences. It actively supports their academic journey, ensuring every student has access to the resources and opportunities needed to succeed.

5.4 AI FOR SPECIAL NEEDS EDUCATION: OPPORTUNITIES AND CHALLENGES

Special needs education presents unique challenges and profound opportunities for applying artificial intelligence. Here, AI's potential to customize educational experiences shines brightly, offering paths to learning that are not merely adapted but fundamentally designed to meet the varied and specific needs of students with disabilities. This approach transcends traditional educational methods, providing a profoundly transformative level of individualization.

Customization for students with special needs involves more than simply adjusting learning speeds or presenting content in various sensory formats. It requires an intricate understanding of each student's unique challenges and abilities, whether they pertain to cognitive, developmental, physical, or emotional aspects. Through detailed data analysis and learning algorithms, AI systems can develop highly specialized educational experiences that cater to these needs. For instance, AI can be programmed to recognize and adapt to the behavioral cues of students with autism, modifying lesson delivery based on the student's current state of focus or stress. Similarly, for students with dyslexia, AI can alter text display, adapt language complexity, and provide interactive, multimodal content that facilitates easier reading and comprehension.

However, the use of AI in special needs education extends beyond adaptive learning systems. Various AI-powered tools and technologies have been specifically developed to enhance accessibility. Text-to-speech software, for example, assists students with visual impairments or reading difficulties. AI-driven applications like these can read text aloud from books, websites, and other educational materials, providing equal access to information. Another significant advancement is AI-powered mobility devices, which can help physically disabled students navigate school environments more independently. These tools are not just about accessibility; they are about empowering students with disabilities, offering them the freedom to explore and interact with their learning environments in previously challenging or impossible ways.

Despite the promising advancements, integrating AI into special services education is challenging. One of the primary concerns is ensuring that these technologies are sensitive to the highly individualized conditions of each student. AI systems must be designed and trained to handle diverse needs with sensitivity and accuracy. Moreover, there is a potential risk of dependency on technology, where students become overly reliant on AI tools, potentially hindering the development of their capabilities or problem-solving skills. Balancing the use of AI with opportunities for students to practice and develop independent skills is crucial.

Collaboration plays a pivotal role in addressing these challenges and in the successful implementation of AI in special needs education. This involves partnerships between AI developers, educators, and particular education specialists who can provide insights into the practical aspects of teaching students with disabilities. These collaborations ensure that AI tools are technically sound, pedagogically practical, and ethically designed. For instance, input from special education teachers can guide AI developers in creating more intuitive and useful applications for students with specific learning disabilities. Such collaborative efforts can lead to innovations that genuinely make educational environments more inclusive.

As we continue to explore the intersection of AI and special needs education, it becomes clear that AI has immense potential to transform learning experiences for students with disabilities. By carefully navigating the challenges and harnessing the opportunities, we can create educational tools that not only compensate for disabilities but actively empower all students to reach their fullest potential.

5.5 FEEDBACK AND ASSESSMENT THROUGH AI: IMMEDIATE AND ACCURATE

In the rapidly evolving educational landscape, Artificial Intelligence (AI) integration has catalyzed a significant transformation in student feedback and assessment. AI systems, designed with sophisticated algorithms, can now provide real-time feedback to students, a development that marks a substantial shift from traditional assessment methods. This capability allows for immediate learning adjustments, which are essential in addressing misconceptions at the moment they occur and reinforcing concepts effectively; when a student interacts with an AI-enhanced learning platform, whether by completing a set of problems or engaging in a simulation, the AI system instantly evaluates their responses and provides feedback. This response clarifies doubts swiftly and helps keep the learning momentum uninterrupted, fostering a dynamic educational experience where students can adapt their learning strategies based on real-time insights.

The precision and objectivity of AI-driven assessments stand out as one of their most significant advantages. Traditional assessment methods, often susceptible to subjective biases and human error, can lead to inconsistencies in evaluating student performance. AI, however, applies consistent criteria to all assessments, ensuring fairness and uniformity in the evaluation process. This objectivity is crucial in educational settings, as it upholds the integrity of assessments and ensures that all students are evaluated based on the same standards. Moreover, AI systems can handle complex data sets and analyze patterns in student responses that might be too subtle for human evaluators to notice. This enhances the accuracy of assessments and provides deeper insights into student learning processes, enabling more targeted educational interventions.

Formative assessment techniques powered by AI are particularly effective in monitoring student progress and understanding throughout the learning process. Unlike summative assessments, which evaluate student learning at the end of an instructional period, formative assessments provide ongoing insights into student progress, allowing educators to adjust instruction in real-time. AI-driven formative assessments can range from adaptive quizzes that adjust their difficulty based on the student's performance to sophisticated systems that analyze open-ended responses for conceptual understanding. These AI-enhanced formative tools continuously collect data on student performance, which is interpreted to provide educators with detailed reports on individual and class-wide progress. This ongoing assessment process is invaluable in creating a responsive learning environment where instructional strategies are continually refined to meet the evolving educational needs of students.

The impact of immediate and accurate feedback on student motivation must be addressed. When students receive instant responses to their actions, it reinforces their understanding and actively engages them in the learning process.

This immediate validation or correction of their answers keeps students invested in the learning activity, enhancing motivation and engagement. Moreover, the precision of AI-driven feedback ensures that students receive accurate information on their performance, which builds their trust in the educational process and encourages them to invest more effort into their learning. Furthermore, personalized feedback makes the learning experience more relevant for students, as they can see how the material applies directly to their skills and areas for improvement. This customized approach makes learning more engaging and effective, as students are more likely to pay attention and put effort into areas that they understand directly impact their personal learning goals.

As we continue to harness the capabilities of AI in education, the potential to enhance how we assess and provide feedback to students is immense. By leveraging AI for immediate, accurate, and personalized feedback, we can create learning environments that are more effective, equitable, and motivating. This shift towards real-time, data-driven feedback mechanisms represents a forward-thinking approach to education, where technology and pedagogy converge to produce the best student outcomes. As educators, embracing these AI-driven assessment tools can transform our teaching practices, making them more aligned with today's learners' dynamic, interactive, and personalized needs.

5.6 SCAFFOLDING LEARNING WITH AI: FROM SUPPORT TO INDEPENDENCE

In education, scaffolding represents a systematic approach whereby instructional support is provided to students in the initial stages of learning and gradually removed as their independence and proficiency grow. This pedagogical strategy is rooted in the idea that learning is most effective when it builds upon what the learner already knows, adjusting in complexity and depth as the learner's capability develops. Artificial Intelligence (AI) has the potential to revolutionize this process by automating and adapting scaffolding in real-time, ensuring that the support provided aligns perfectly with the student's evolving needs.

AI-driven systems excel in creating dynamic educational environments where scaffolding can be precisely calibrated and seamlessly integrated into learning paths. These systems analyze continuous feedback from student activities, gauging their understanding and adjusting the support accordingly. For instance, when a student demonstrates a solid grasp of a concept, AI can introduce more complex materials, challenging the student to apply their knowledge in broader contexts. Conversely, if a student struggles, the AI can reintroduce foundational concepts or simplify the information, ensuring the student feels safe and can achieve success at a manageable pace.

The gradual release of responsibility is a core component of AI-enhanced scaffolding. Initially, AI systems provide substantial guidance, breaking tasks into manageable steps and offering hints and cues. AI support is strategically reduced as students progress, encouraging learners to take greater initiative. This method fosters a sense of achievement and confidence among students as they recognize their growing ability to tackle complex problems independently. Moreover, AI systems can personalize the pace at which responsibility is transferred, accommodating the unique learning speeds of individual students, which is often a challenge in traditional educational settings.

AI also facilitates the creation of personalized learning journeys that effectively scaffold learning for each student by integrating data from various sources—previous performance, pace of learning, preferred content delivery modes—AI crafts unique learning pathways that adapt over time. This personalization ensures that each student experiences a learning journey that is aligned with their academic needs and resonates with their learning preferences and goals.

Real-world applications of AI-enabled scaffolding are demonstrating significant benefits in diverse educational settings. For example, in a middle school math class, an AI system was used for scaffolding learning for students with varying proficiency levels. The AI provided real-time adjustments to the learning content, offering more detailed explanations and interactive problems to students who needed more support while presenting challenging scenarios to those who were ready to advance. This approach allowed every student to progress appropriately, significantly improving their engagement and understanding of mathematical concepts.

Another instance involved a language learning app that used AI to scaffold vocabulary acquisition for non-native speakers. The app initially presented new words with visual aids and contextual sentences, gradually reducing these supports as the learner's familiarity with the vocabulary increased. The AI monitored the learner's recall and comprehension, adjusting the frequency and complexity of review sessions to optimize learning retention. This personalized scaffolding helped learners build confidence and proficiency in the new language more effectively than traditional study methods.

These examples highlight how AI can transform the scaffolding process, making it more dynamic, responsive, and tailored to individual learners. By leveraging AI to support and gradually foster independence in learners, educators can create more effective, engaging, and personalized educational experiences that encourage students to become confident, autonomous learners.

As we conclude this exploration of AI's role in scaffolding learning, it is clear that the potential of AI to enhance educational outcomes through personalized support is immense. By providing adaptive, precisely calibrated assistance, AI empowers students to take ownership of their learning, progressing at their own pace and according to their needs. This chapter not only reaffirms the transformative impact of AI on traditional teaching methodologies but also sets the stage for further discussions on integrating AI in various educational scenarios, ensuring that all students have the tools and support necessary to succeed in an increasingly complex world. As we move forward, the next chapter will delve into how AI is reshaping the landscape of educational assessment, opening new avenues for measuring and enhancing student learning through innovative, technology-driven approaches.

6

PROFESSIONAL DEVELOPMENT AND LIFELONG LEARNING WITH AI

Education is no exception in a world where the only constant is change. The rapid integration of Artificial Intelligence (AI) into various sectors, especially education, necessitates a parallel evolution in professional development for educators. Imagine a scenario where every teacher, regardless of their initial comfort with technology, is adept at leveraging AI to enhance their teaching methods and learning processes. This isn't just an ideal; it's quickly becoming an imperative. As we explore the profound impact of AI on professional development, it's crucial to understand not just the opportunities but also the tailored approaches that AI makes possible for educators' growth.

6.1 AI AS A TOOL FOR TEACHER TRAINING AND PROFESSIONAL DEVELOPMENT

AI's role in redefining professional development extends beyond mere automation, venturing into customization, simulation, and real-time enhancement of teaching skills.

More personalized experiences are replacing the traditional one-size-fits-all approach to professional development, thanks to AI's ability to tailor learning to individual educator's needs. AI systems can identify specific areas where each teacher excels or needs improvement by analyzing data on educators' teaching styles, subject knowledge, and student feedback. This personalized approach ensures that professional development is a routine exercise and a meaningful growth journey. For instance, an AI system might suggest that a veteran literature teacher refine question-posing techniques to enhance student engagement while recommending that a novice math teacher focus on classroom management strategies.

Simulation and Modeling

One of the most innovative applications of AI in teacher training is the use of simulations and scenario-based learning. These AI-driven simulations provide a risk-free environment for teachers to practice and hone their skills. For example, an AI simulation might create a virtual classroom setting where a teacher can experiment with different pedagogical approaches to see how hypothetical students might respond. These scenarios range from managing a disruptive class to integrating new technology into a lesson plan. The essential advantage here is its safety net; educators can test various strategies and learn from mistakes without impacting real students, boosting their confidence and competence in handling diverse classroom situations.

Real-time Feedback and Assessment

The immediate feedback provided by AI during these training sessions is invaluable. Unlike traditional workshops, where feedback can be delayed and may no longer be relevant, AI systems offer instant responses to teachers' actions in simulations. This real-time critique allows educators to understand and rectify their mistakes immediately, embedding effective teaching practices. Furthermore, AI-driven assessments during these sessions can help track progress over time, offering insights into how teachers improve and where they might still need to focus their development efforts.

Continuous Professional Growth

Perhaps most importantly, AI facilitates a continuous learning loop for educators. AI tools are constantly updated with the latest research and data on effective teaching strategies and educational standards. These resources ensure teachers remain at the cutting edge of educational methodologies. Moreover, AI systems can recommend timely microcourses or updates based on the latest educational trends, new state standards, or emerging student needs. This ongoing process of learning and adaptation is crucial in an era where educational paradigms shift rapidly due to technological advancements.

By integrating AI into professional development, we are not just enhancing the way educators learn; we are transforming them into lifelong learners who are continuously evolving. This shift is vital in preparing educators to meet the challenges of today's diverse and dynamic classrooms and embrace the possibilities of tomorrow's learning environments.

6.2 LIFELONG LEARNING FOR EDUCATORS THROUGH AI-ENHANCED COURSES

In an era where the boundaries of time and space are increasingly blurred in education, AI-enhanced courses emerge as a beacon for educators striving to balance their professional responsibilities with personal growth. These courses are meticulously designed to be accessed from anywhere at any time, embodying the true spirit of flexibility. Imagine engaging in a nuanced lecture on educational psychology or participating in a real-time AI-driven workshop from the comfort of your home or during a break in your school day. This level of accessibility is revolutionary, not only in how it redefines when and where learning occurs but also in ensuring that opportunities for professional development are not tethered to physical presence or traditional school hours.

Moreover, the dynamic nature of educational demands and standards calls for content that is not static but evolves. AI-enhanced courses excel by integrating systems designed to update content continuously. Algorithms analyze emerging educational trends and new research to update course materials, ensuring that what you learn is not outdated but is cutting-edge and relevant. This feature is pivotal, particularly in fields like educational technology, where new tools and methodologies are constantly being developed. Through AI, these courses adapt to include the latest insights, offering you a learning experience that is as current as it is comprehensive.

Interactive content is another cornerstone of AI-enhanced courses that transforms passive learning into an active, engaging process. Through elements such as interactive simulations, real-time quizzes, and collaborative projects, these courses ensure that your learning experience is not only informative but also engaging and engaging with complex simulations that model classroom management scenarios, for instance, allows you to apply theoretical knowledge in a virtual environment, enhancing your understanding through practice. Similarly, AI-driven quizzes provide instant feedback, helping you to assess your knowledge and identify areas for improvement immediately. The inclusion of collaborative projects facilitated by AI also encourages peer interaction, which needs to be included in traditional online learning environments. These projects allow you to work with fellow educators from around the globe, sharing insights and strategies, thus enriching your learning experience.

Tracking progress and managing certifications efficiently is another advantage AI offers in these courses. AI systems meticulously track your progress through each course, analyzing data from your performance to provide personalized insights into your learning patterns. This information can be instrumental in guiding your future learning paths, suggesting areas where you might need to focus more or new topics you find stimulating. Furthermore, these systems manage certifications, maintaining a detailed record of the courses you have completed and the skills you have acquired. This helps build your professional portfolio and demonstrate your commitment to continuous professional development, a crucial aspect in the ever-evolving field of education.

Through these AI-enhanced courses, the landscape of educator professional development is transformed. They offer a flexible, dynamic, and engaging learning experience meticulously tailored to meet the needs of modern educators. As these courses evolve, they promise to play a pivotal role in shaping a new era of educational excellence where learning is continuous, accessible, and profoundly empowering.

6.3 DEVELOPING AI LITERACY AMONG EDUCATIONAL STAFF

In the ever-evolving landscape of education, where Artificial Intelligence (AI) increasingly plays a pivotal role, equipping educators with a solid understanding of AI fundamentals is critical. This foundational knowledge empowers you, the educator, to harness AI's potential effectively within your teaching practices and beyond. First, a fundamental grasp of AI involves understanding its key concepts and terminology. At its core, AI refers to systems or machines that mimic human intelligence to perform tasks and can improve themselves based on the information they collect. Concepts such as machine learning, neural networks, natural language processing, and robotics form the backbone of AI. Machine learning, for instance, enables computers to learn from and make decisions based on data without being explicitly programmed. Inspired by the human brain, neural networks help machines recognize patterns and make sense of complex data sets. Familiarity with these terms and concepts is the first step in demystifying AI and appreciating its educational applications.

Beyond theoretical understanding, practical AI applications in the educational sphere bring these concepts to life. AI tools are not just about automating administrative tasks but are increasingly integral in personalizing learning experiences, assessing student progress in real-time, and providing data-driven insights that guide educational strategies. For instance, AI-driven analytics can help identify students who might benefit from additional support in specific areas, enabling timely and targeted interventions. Understanding these applications illustrates how AI can enhance your effectiveness as an educator, making your interactions with students more informed and impactful.

Structured workshops and training modules ensure educational staff can proficiently navigate and utilize AI tools. These training sessions should focus on the technical operation of AI tools and their strategic integration into teaching and learning processes. Formats could vary from hands-on workshops that allow you to interact directly with AI software and systems to scenario-based modules to explore how AI can be applied in real-world educational settings. These learning opportunities should be designed to cater to varying levels of prior AI knowledge, ensuring inclusivity and accessibility for all educators. Additionally, incorporating collaborative learning approaches in these sessions can be particularly beneficial, as they allow you to learn from and with your peers, fostering an environment of collective growth and innovation.

Assessing AI competency among educational staff is equally crucial to ensure these technologies are integrated effectively and ethically in academic settings. This assessment can be achieved through regular evaluations that measure your ability to use AI tools and understand when and why to use them. Such assessments could be integrated into the professional development programs, providing ongoing checkpoints that help gauge your progress and identify areas for further learning. Moreover, these assessments help maintain a standard of AI literacy within educational institutions, ensuring that all educators have the knowledge and skills necessary to adapt to the increasingly AI-infused educational landscape.

By fostering a robust understanding of AI among educational staff, we lay a foundational pillar that supports the adoption of new technologies and the continuous evolution of academic practices. This endeavor enhances individual teaching effectiveness and collectively elevates the educational institution's capability to meet the needs of today's and tomorrow's learners. As AI continues to transform the academic landscape, your role as an educator is not just to adapt to these changes but to actively participate in shaping how AI is integrated into learning, ensuring it serves the best interests of all students.

6.4 | PEER COLLABORATION AND AI: LEARNING FROM GLOBAL BEST PRACTICES

In the expansive arena of education, where challenges are as diverse as the global community they affect, the power of collaboration cannot be understated. Artificial Intelligence

(AI) is a formidable ally, bridging geographical and linguistic divides and connecting educators worldwide. Such connectivity is not just about sharing ideas; it's about creating a vibrant, dynamic forum where best practices and innovative teaching methods are discussed, actively exchanged, and implemented. The potential for AI to foster global learning communities is immense. Through platforms that incorporate AI, educators can participate in virtual exchanges, engaging in discussions and collaborative projects with peers from different educational systems and cultural backgrounds. This global interaction enriches the teaching experience, exposing educators to various pedagogical strategies and educational challenges worldwide.

AI-powered collaboration tools are instrumental in facilitating these interactions. Real-time translation services, for example, break down language barriers that have traditionally impeded international collaboration. An educator in Japan can share innovative techniques in mathematics education with a counterpart in Brazil, with AI seamlessly translating the exchange, ensuring both parties derive maximum benefit from the interaction. Furthermore, AI-driven recommendation systems can enhance these collaborations by suggesting resources, contacts, and content most relevant to the users' interests and needs. Such systems analyze user data to identify patterns and preferences, tailoring recommendations enriching the collaborative experience and ensuring educators receive useful, context-specific information.

Case Studies of Successful Collaborations

Consider the case of an international project in which teachers from Sweden and Kenya collaborated to develop a curriculum that integrates environmental science with sustainable development. AI tools facilitated their collaboration by providing platforms for real-time communication and data exchange and by offering predictive analytics to gauge the effectiveness of their proposed teaching strategies. The success of this project not only improved educational outcomes in both regions but also demonstrated how AI can be pivotal in transcending traditional boundaries to foster meaningful educational collaborations.

Another example involves a joint venture between educators in Canada and South Africa, focusing on using AI to enhance literacy among elementary students. Through a shared AI platform, teachers could develop and refine a series of interactive, gamified learning modules tailored to the needs of their diverse student populations. The AI system provided ongoing feedback on student performance and engagement, allowing educators to continuously improve the modules for greater effectiveness. The collaborative effort resulted in significant improvements in student literacy rates and highlighted the potential for AI to facilitate adaptive learning in a cross-cultural context.

Building a Culture of Collaboration

Creating a culture that embraces collaboration requires more than just providing the tools for interaction. It necessitates a foundational shift in how educational institutions and educators view professional development and knowledge sharing. Cultivating this culture includes promoting policies that encourage collaborative projects and recognizing contributions made through cooperative efforts. Academic leaders can foster an environment that values teamwork and shared learning by integrating collaborative projects into their school's key performance indicators.

Furthermore, professional development programs can incorporate training on how to effectively use AI tools for collaboration, ensuring that educators are willing and able to engage in international partnerships. Schools can establish partnerships with tech companies to provide educators access to the latest AI tools and training, equipping them with the skills necessary to participate in and benefit from global learning networks. By embedding collaboration in the professional development narrative, educators are encouraged to seek out and contribute to collective knowledge, driving the educational innovation our globalized world necessitates.

These initiatives reshape the educational landscape to be more inclusive, interconnected, and innovative. AI supports the logistical aspects of collaboration and inspires a shift in educational paradigms, where learning and teaching are viewed as dynamic, global, and collaborative enterprises. As we continue to harness AI's capabilities, the boundaries of what we can achieve in education expand, paving the way for a future where collaborative learning and teaching across borders are not just possible but are standard practice, enriching the educational experiences of teachers and students alike.

6.5 LEADING AI INITIATIVES: SKILLS FOR THE EDUCATOR AS A CHANGE AGENT

In educational transformation, educators are not merely adopters of Artificial Intelligence (AI) but pivotal in steering its integration within their institutions. The ability to lead AI initiatives effectively demands vision, strategic planning, and proactive stakeholder engagement. As an educator, your role expands beyond imparting knowledge; you become a change agent, orchestrating the seamless incorporation of AI into educational practices.

Leadership in AI Integration

Leading AI integration begins with vision-setting. It's about crafting a clear, compelling vision that not only aligns with the educational goals of your institution but also illustrates the profound impact AI can have on teaching and learning processes. This vision should encapsulate how AI can personalize student learning, enhance educational access, and streamline administrative tasks, freeing teachers to focus more on pedagogy. Strategic planning is the next critical step. This involves laying out a detailed roadmap for AI adoption, which includes setting achievable milestones, identifying necessary resources, and establishing timelines. Your strategic plan should also encompass the development of policies and guidelines that address the use of AI in your school, ensuring that its integration is ethical and practical.

Engaging stakeholders is one of the most crucial aspects of leading AI initiatives. This process involves informing and actively involving teachers, students, parents, and administrative staff in the AI integration process. Regular meetings, workshops, and feedback sessions can be instrumental in this regard, as they provide platforms for stakeholders to voice their concerns, offer suggestions, and directly contribute to the implementation process. Effective stakeholder engagement facilitates smoother adoption by addressing potential resistance and enriches the initiative with diverse perspectives, enhancing the likelihood of its success.

Change Management

Introducing AI in educational settings invariably brings about change, which can often be met with apprehension or resistance. As an educator leading AI initiatives, I know it is essential to manage this change adeptly. One effective strategy is to start small and implement AI in phases. Begin with pilot projects that allow stakeholders to witness first-hand the benefits of AI, such as an AI-driven tutor or analytics program. These early successes can help build confidence and buy-in for broader AI adoption.

Training colleagues is another vital aspect of change management. Professional development sessions tailored to AI literacy and application equip teachers with the necessary skills and demystify AI, making it more accessible and less intimidating. These training sessions should be practical and hands-on, allowing teachers to interact directly with AI tools and explore their potential applications in a supportive environment. Addressing resistance to AI involves open communication and transparency. Regularly updating stakeholders about the progress of AI initiatives and the challenges encountered helps maintain trust. It's also important to be receptive to feedback and ready to adjust AI strategies in response to stakeholder concerns.

Advocacy for Ethical AI Use

As AI becomes more embedded in educational processes, advocating for its ethical use is imperative. This involves ensuring that AI tools are used in ways that are fair, transparent, and beneficial to all students. It means being vigilant about issues such as data privacy, bias in AI algorithms, and the potential for AI to widen educational disparities. As an educator, you play a crucial role in championing these ethical considerations within your institution and the broader academic community.

Your advocacy can extend to participating in forums and panels on AI ethics, contributing to academic papers, or leading community outreach programs that educate the public about the ethical dimensions of AI in education. By being a vocal advocate for responsible AI use, you help shape policies and practices prioritizing student welfare and equity, ensuring that AI is a tool for enhancing educational outcomes rather than creating new divides.

Networking and Influence

Building networks with other AI-driven educators and influencers can amplify your impact as a change agent. These networks provide valuable opportunities for sharing resources, strategies, and insights on AI integration. They also offer a support system that can be instrumental in navigating the complexities of AI adoption. Networking can extend beyond local or national boundaries, involving international collaborations that expose you to global best practices and innovative approaches in AI education.

Leveraging AI-driven data and success stories is an effective way to influence decision-makers within and beyond your institution. Data on improved student outcomes, increased efficiency, and enhanced learning experiences make compelling cases for expanding AI initiatives. Coupled with personal narratives and testimonials from students and teachers who have directly benefited from AI, these data points can be persuasive tools in securing the support and resources needed for larger-scale AI projects.

As you lead AI initiatives within your educational setting, your role encompasses being a visionary, a strategist, a communicator, an advocate, and a network builder. This multifaceted responsibility not only enhances your professional capabilities but also sets the foundation for a future where education is more inclusive, personalized, and efficient.

6.6 EVALUATING AND SELECTING PROFESSIONAL DEVELOPMENT AI TOOLS

In an era of rapid technological advances, selecting the right AI tools for professional development requires a nuanced approach, ensuring that these technologies align well with educational goals and deliver substantial value. To navigate this complex landscape, it is vital to establish clear criteria that guide the selection process. These criteria should encompass the educational impact of the AI tools and their usability, cost-effectiveness, and alignment with professional standards. A tool's educational impact is the most critical criterion, as it directly affects the learning outcomes. This involves evaluating whether the AI application enhances understanding, supports skill development, and integrates effectively into existing educational frameworks. Usability is another essential factor, as tools that are difficult to navigate can become barriers to effective learning rather than facilitators. Therefore, an ideal AI tool should feature an intuitive interface and be accessible to educators with varying levels of tech proficiency.

Cost-effectiveness is another pivotal aspect, especially in educational environments where budget constraints are often prevalent. The benefits of an AI tool must justify its cost, not just in terms of monetary expenditure but also in terms of the time educators invest to learn and implement it. Lastly, alignment with professional standards ensures that the AI tools adhere to the ethical, legal, and professional norms prevalent in the educational sector. This alignment safeguards institutions against potential legal or ethical breaches and enhances the credibility and relevance of professional development efforts.

Vendor Evaluation

Selecting the right vendor is critical as it determines the quality and reliability of the AI tools. Evaluating vendors involves several vital considerations, starting with their reputation. A vendor with a robust track record of providing high-quality, reliable AI solutions to educational institutions is likelier to offer products that meet high standards. Support services are another crucial factor. Vendors should offer comprehensive technical support and training resources to assist educators in implementing and utilizing AI tools effectively. User reviews can also provide valuable insights into the experiences of other institutions with the vendor's products, highlighting potential strengths and weaknesses.

Trial and Feedback

Implementing a trial-and-feedback approach allows educational institutions to test AI tools in real-world settings before committing to full adoption. This phase is crucial for assessing how well the tool integrates with existing systems and meets the educational needs. Gathering detailed feedback from all users, including teachers, administrators, and IT staff, is essential during the trial. This feedback should cover aspects such as the tool's impact on learning outcomes, ease of use, and any technical issues encountered. Based on this feedback, institutions can make informed decisions about whether to proceed with full implementation, abandon the tool, or seek modifications from the vendor.

Continuous Evaluation

Once an AI tool is integrated into professional development programs, continuous evaluation is essential to ensure it remains effective over time. This ongoing assessment involves regularly reviewing the tool's impact on teaching and learning, staying updated with the latest AI advancements, and soliciting continuous user feedback. Changes in educational standards or technological advancements may necessitate updates or modifications to the AI tools to keep them relevant and effective. Additionally, continuous evaluation helps identify new needs or challenges that may emerge among educators, allowing institutions to adjust their professional development strategies accordingly.

By adhering to these guidelines—establishing clear selection criteria, conducting thorough vendor evaluations, utilizing a trial and feedback approach, and committing to continuous assessment—educational institutions can make informed decisions that maximize the benefits of AI in professional development. This strategic approach not only enhances the quality of education but also ensures that investments in AI yield substantial, enduring returns, empowering educators to meet current and future challenges.

As we conclude this exploration of how to evaluate and select AI tools for professional development effectively, it becomes evident that a thoughtful, structured approach is essential for harnessing the full potential of these technologies. By carefully selecting tools that align with educational goals, continuously assessing their impact, and remaining adaptable to new developments, academic institutions can ensure that their investment in AI enhances professional development and contributes to a higher standard of education. This proactive stance prepares educators not just to adapt to changes brought about by AI but to actively shape these transformations, ensuring that they positively impact learning outcomes and teaching practices. As we progress into the next chapter, we will delve deeper into the future trends in AI in education, exploring how these evolving technologies are anticipated to transform the educational landscape further, presenting both new opportunities and challenges.

7

ENGAGING AND MOTIVATING STUDENTS WITH AI

In the evolving landscape of education, the quest to captivate and inspire every student remains paramount. Imagine entering a classroom where each lesson is not just a transfer of knowledge but a captivating journey tailored to engage every student's curiosity and drive. This is the transformative potential of AI-driven gamification in education. This strategy educates, deeply engages, and motivates students by weaving essential learning outcomes with the compelling elements of game design. Integrating these innovative strategies into your teaching, you're not merely instructing but inspiring a new generation of learners equipped to navigate and excel in a complex world.

7.1 GAMIFICATION OF LEARNING THROUGH AI

Introduction to Educational Gamification

Gamification in an educational context involves applying game-design elements in learning environments to increase student engagement and motivation. This approach taps into the intrinsic human love for games, transforming routine educational tasks into exciting and enjoyable activities. By integrating elements such as point scoring, competition, and rules of play, gamification goes beyond traditional learning paradigms, making the educational process both stimulating and enjoyable.

Artificial Intelligence enhances these gamification strategies by personalizing the gaming elements to align with individual students' learning styles and progress. AI algorithms analyze student data to tailor challenges, adjust difficulty levels, and provide real-time feedback, ensuring the gamified learning experiences are fun and highly effective. The beauty of AI in gamification lies in its ability to make learning profoundly personal and responsive, adapting in real-time to meet each student's evolving educational needs.

AI-Driven Game Mechanics

Specific AI-driven game mechanics amplify student engagement and motivation, such as adaptive challenges, rewards systems, and progress tracking. Adaptive challenges are efficient because they adjust the difficulty of tasks based on the student's performance, ensuring that every student finds the tasks neither too easy nor too difficult. This dynamic adjustment helps maintain an optimal learning zone and motivates students through just-right challenges.

The rewards systems in gamification, powered by AI, personalize student incentives. For instance, AI can determine what rewards motivate a student the most—virtual badges, unlocking levels, or gaining access to new learning content—and integrate these into their learning pathways. Moreover, progress tracking facilitated by AI provides students and educators with visible metrics of improvement and achievement, reinforcing the student's sense of accomplishment and encouraging them to set and reach new goals.

Integration with Curriculum

Integrating gamification seamlessly into the curriculum is crucial. It must enrich the learning experience and maintain the educational goals. To achieve this, identify specific learning objectives that lend themselves well to gamification. For example, language vocabulary or historical facts, which require memorization and recall, can be effectively learned through quiz-based games.

When implementing gamification, ensuring that the game elements are closely aligned with the educational content is essential. The AI can assist by mapping game mechanics to curriculum requirements, ensuring that every aspect of the game serves a clear academic purpose. This careful integration ensures that the gamification strategy completes the learning objectives rather than overshadowing them.

Case Studies and Outcomes

One illustrative case study of successful gamification in education involved a middle school history class where students learned about ancient civilizations through a quest-based game. The game, powered by AI, adapted quests to each student's learning pace and provided personalized puzzles and challenges based on their progress. The outcome was remarkable; students achieved higher scores on their history tests and reported greater enjoyment and engagement in learning about historical events.

Another example comes from a high school math class where an AI-driven platform gamified the process of solving algebra problems. Students earned points and badges for solving equations and could use these points to customize avatars or unlock advanced challenges. This approach made learning algebra more engaging, allowing students to track their progress and visually understand their learning journey.

These cases exemplify how gamification, when enhanced by AI, can transform educational experiences, making learning both enjoyable and effective. As you consider integrating these strategies into your curriculum, remember that the ultimate goal is to enhance engagement and motivation, turning every learning opportunity into an inviting challenge students are eager to tackle. This approach fosters a love for learning and prepares students with the resilience and curiosity needed to thrive in their educational pursuits and beyond.

7.2 VIRTUAL REALITY AND AI: CREATING IMMERSIVE LEARNING EXPERIENCES

Basics of AI-Enhanced Virtual Reality

Virtual Reality (VR) is a modern educational frontier, offering immersive environments that revolutionize traditional learning. At its core, VR involves using computer technology to create a simulated environment similar to or completely different from the real world. Users are immersed in an artificial digital environment that they can interact with using devices such as headsets or multi-projected setups. AI enhances these VR environments by introducing elements of adaptability and personalization, making them more than static simulations. AI algorithms process data from user interactions within the VR environment in real-time, allowing the system to adjust experiences better to suit individual learning needs and preferences. For instance, if a student struggles with a specific virtual lab procedure, AI can modify the difficulty level or provide tailored guidance to facilitate understanding. This dynamic interactivity ensures that VR is not merely a technological novelty but a potent, adaptive educational tool.

The integration of AI into VR goes beyond mere personalization; it transforms VR into an intelligent tutor capable of responding to subtle cues from the user. This might include adjusting the pacing of a lesson based on the user's engagement levels or providing additional resources when a user shows interest in a particular topic. Such capabilities make AI-enhanced VR an exceptional tool in the educator's toolkit, offering experiences that are not only immersive but also inherently responsive to the learner's needs.

Applications in Various Disciplines

AI-enhanced VR finds profound applications across diverse educational disciplines, each offering unique opportunities for immersive learning. In history education, AI-enhanced VR can transport students back in time, allowing them to explore ancient civilizations or significant historical events firsthand. Imagine students walking through the Roman Forum at the height of the Roman Empire or witnessing the signing of the Declaration of Independence. These vivid, interactive experiences make history palpable, fostering a deeper understanding and retention of historical knowledge.

In science education, AI-enhanced VR can simulate complex experiments or phenomena that would be too dangerous, expensive, or impractical to experience in a traditional class-room. Students can manipulate molecular structures, observe chemical reactions at a molecular level, or explore the vastness of space, all within a safe and controlled virtual environment. This hands-on approach demystifies complex scientific concepts and ignites curiosity and passion for the sciences.

The arts also benefit immensely from AI-enhanced VR, offering a new creative expression and exploration medium. Art students can create and walk through their three-dimensional art pieces, experiment with virtual materials, or study masterpieces up close without the constraints of physical museums. This immersive interaction with art enriches the learning experience, providing a canvas limited only by imagination.

Benefits to Student Engagement

The psychological and educational benefits of immersive learning experiences facilitated by AI-enhanced VR are significant. Firstly, the immersive nature of VR generates a sense of presence and involvement that is difficult to achieve through traditional learning methods. This heightened engagement is crucial in maintaining students' attention and interest, particularly in subjects students might find challenging or unengaging. Secondly, VR experiences have been shown to enhance retention rates. The multisensory engagement in VR experiences leads to better recall and understanding of the information, a principle rooted in the cognitive theory of multimedia learning, which posits that people learn better from words and pictures than from words alone.

Moreover, AI-enhanced VR can adapt to provide scaffolded learning experiences that support students at various proficiency levels, ensuring that each learner is adequately challenged but not overwhelmed. This personalized learning journey improves educational outcomes and boosts students' confidence in their abilities, fostering a positive attitude toward learning.

Implementation Challenges and Solutions

Despite the benefits, implementing AI-enhanced VR in education is challenging. The high costs of VR hardware and the technological infrastructure required to support such systems can be a significant barrier, particularly for under-resourced schools. To address these challenges, educators can explore funding options such as grants, partnerships with technology companies, or crowdfunding campaigns to enhance technological access. Schools can also start with smaller-scale implementations, using mobile-based VR solutions that are generally less expensive and require minimal equipment.

Another challenge is the potential for technological intimidation among students and educators. To mitigate this, comprehensive training sessions for educators are essential. These sessions should not only cover the technical aspects of using VR but also pedagogical strategies to integrate VR effectively into the curriculum. For students, introductory sessions that allow them to familiarize themselves with VR interfaces can alleviate anxieties and encourage open-minded engagement with the technology.

In conclusion, as you embark on incorporating AI-enhanced VR into your educational practices, the journey promises to transform how students learn and how they perceive and interact with the world. Through careful planning, collaboration, and a commitment to overcoming challenges, AI-enhanced VR can provide deeply engaging and profoundly transformative learning experiences, preparing students for a future where digital and physical realities converge.

7.3 AI AND THE CHALLENGE OF STUDENT ENGAGEMENT IN ONLINE LEARNING

Online learning environments offer unparalleled flexibility and accessibility, allowing education to reach beyond the traditional classroom walls. However, they also introduce specific challenges, particularly in maintaining student engagement. With the physical presence of peers and instructors, students may feel safe, their attention may wane, and their motivation may diminish over time. Identifying these engagement issues is the first step toward crafting effective solutions. Artificial Intelligence (AI) plays a pivotal role by analyzing data on student behaviors, such as login frequency, assignment submission times, and interaction rates with learning materials. These metrics provide invaluable insights, revealing patterns that signify disengagement, such as sporadic participation or prolonged inactivity.

AI's capability to analyze such extensive data allows for the early identification of disengaged students, enabling timely intervention strategies. For instance, automated alerts can be triggered if AI detects a student's interaction with course materials significantly decreased over two consecutive weeks. These alerts prompt instructors to reach out personally, via a video call or personalized messages, to re-engage the student and address any underlying issues. This proactive approach ensures that students stay on track with their educational commitments, feeling overlooked or unsupported.

Moreover, AI tools that enhance engagement in online learning environments transform educational experiences. Interactive AI tutors, for instance, provide real-time academic assistance and personalized learning experiences. These tutors use natural language processing to understand student queries and respond with explanations, hints, or additional learning resources. Their availability around the clock ensures that students receive immediate help whenever needed, mirroring the ever-accessible nature of online learning. Additionally, AI-driven chatbots can facilitate administrative tasks, answering frequently asked questions about course logistics, deadlines, or grading policies, thereby reducing potential frustrations and keeping students focused on learning.

Analytics tools, another facet of AI's arsenal, customize learning paths by adapting content based on the student's progress and preferences. These tools analyze how students interact with different types of content and learning activities, which provides educators with insights into what works best for each student. For instance, if a student engages more with visual content than text-based materials, the AI system can automatically present upcoming topics using more diagrams, videos, and infographics. This tailored approach maintains the student's interest and caters to their learning style, enhancing engagement and educational outcomes.

Building a sense of community is crucial in online learning environments to counteract feelings of isolation. AI can significantly contribute by facilitating group interactions and collaborative projects. Through data analysis, AI can group students with similar interests or complementary strengths, fostering an environment ripe for collaboration. AI-powered tools can manage and facilitate projects within these groups by setting milestones, scheduling virtual meetups, and mediating discussions. For example, AI can prompt discussion points based on the project's progress or upcoming deadlines, ensuring the group's collaboration is productive and goal-oriented.

Feedback Loops

Continuous feedback is a cornerstone of effective learning, and AI significantly enhances this in online environments. AI systems provide educators with continuous insights into student progress through detailed dashboards that track engagement levels, learning patterns, and assessment performances. This constant data stream allows educators to adjust their teaching strategies in real-time. If a particular module sees lower engagement rates, an instructor can introduce interactive elements or real-time quizzes to revive interest and participation. This dynamic approach to teaching, powered by ongoing AI analysis, ensures that educational strategies remain fluid and responsive to students' needs, keeping them engaged and invested in their learning journey.

Through these AI-driven strategies, online education transcends traditional limitations, offering a responsive, engaging, and community-focused learning experience. As educators continue to leverage AI's capabilities, the potential to transform online learning into a richly interactive and supportive educational environment grows, promising to maintain and enhance student engagement and motivation across digital platforms.

7.4 USING AI TO ENHANCE GROUP PROJECTS AND TEAM COLLABORATION

In the collaborative landscape of modern education, Artificial Intelligence (AI) emerges as a vital ally in optimizing team formation and enhancing group dynamics. By leveraging AI, educators can strategically form student teams with compositions tailored to balance skill sets and align learning styles and educational needs. This optimization enhances group synergy and improves project outcomes, as students are paired in ways that complement each other's strengths and address potential weaknesses.

AI algorithms can analyze individual student data, including past academic performance, preferred learning methods, and personality traits, to assemble diverse yet compatible groups. For example, an AI system might place a student with strong analytical skills but weaker presentation skills with another who excels in communication. This balances the team's competencies and encourages peer-to-peer learning, where students can learn from each other's strengths. The process does not stop at formation; AI continuously learns from group interactions and project outcomes to refine its team-building strategies. This ongoing optimization ensures that groups are well-matched and dynamic, adapting to students' evolving educational journeys.

AI-powered tools play a crucial role in facilitating collaboration within these groups. Shared digital workspaces and AI-mediated communication platforms allow team members to interact seamlessly, regardless of physical location. These platforms can integrate various AI tools, such as real-time document editing, shared resource libraries, and interactive timelines, all of which help streamline collaboration. AI can also assist in scheduling by synchronizing calendars and proposing meeting times that suit all members, thus reducing the administrative overhead often associated with group projects.

Monitoring group dynamics is another area where AI can significantly contribute. By analyzing communication patterns and project progress, AI systems can identify signs of dysfunction, such as uneven participation or conflicts within the group. This monitoring allows educators to intervene early, guiding students to resolve disputes and encouraging quieter group members to participate more fully. For instance, if an AI system notices that one student dominates the conversation in shared digital workspaces, it can prompt the team leader or the instructor to encourage more equitable participation, ensuring that all voices are heard and valued.

Evaluating group work often poses challenges, particularly in assessing individual contributions fairly. AI comes to the forefront in providing solutions that ensure objective and detailed evaluations. Through AI tools, educators can track individual contributions to group projects through written documents, creative contributions, or participation in discussions. This tracking enables a fair assessment of each student's input, ensuring that grades reflect personal effort and group success. Moreover, AI can provide personalized feedback to each student based on their contributions, highlighting strengths and areas for improvement. This customized feedback is crucial for academic growth and personal development as students learn to navigate team dynamics and collaborative challenges.

Through these AI-enhanced strategies, group projects transform from mere academic tasks to rich, collaborative experiences that mirror the complexities of real-world teamwork. By harnessing AI in team formation, project collaboration, group dynamics monitoring, and fair evaluation, educators can significantly enhance the educational value of group projects, preparing students for academic success and for a future where teamwork and collaboration are paramount.

7.5 AI TOOLS FOR STUDENT FEEDBACK: INSTANT AND PERSONALIZED RESPONSES

In the quest to enhance the learning experience, Artificial Intelligence (AI) offers a profound advantage by providing instant feedback to students. This functionality transforms the traditional learning feedback loop, where students typically wait hours or even days to receive responses to queries or submissions. AI dramatically changes this dynamic by analyzing and responding to real-time student inputs. Imagine a student working on a complex algebra problem and getting stuck on a specific step. Instead of floundering or waiting for the next class to seek clarification, AI intervenes immediately, offering hints or directing the student to relevant learning resources. This instant feedback mechanism is pivotal in sustaining the learning momentum and fostering an environment where students feel continuously supported in their learning journeys.

The capability of AI to provide immediate corrections and suggestions is complemented by its ability to personalize this feedback. By leveraging data on individual student performance, learning pace, and historical interactions, AI tailors its responses to the specific needs of each student. For instance, if a student consistently struggles with a particular concept, AI can detect this pattern and adjust its feedback by simplifying explanations or providing additional examples and practice opportunities. This personalized approach ensures that feedback is timely, relevant, and uniquely suited to each student's learning trajectory. Such customization makes learning more effective by addressing individual challenges and reinforcing material in ways that resonate with each student's specific learning needs.

The impact of instant and personalized feedback on student motivation cannot be overstated. When students receive immediate responses to their actions, it reinforces their understanding and actively engages them in the learning process. This immediate validation or correction of their answers keeps students invested in the learning activity, enhancing motivation and engagement. Moreover, the precision of AI-driven feedback ensures that students receive accurate information on their performance, which builds their trust in the educational process and encourages them to invest more effort into their learning. Furthermore, personalized feedback makes the learning experience more relevant for students, as they can see how the material applies directly to their skills and areas for improvement. This customized approach makes learning more engaging and effective, as students are more likely to pay attention and put effort into areas that they understand directly impact their personal learning goals.

Integration of AI tools into assessment processes further streamlines the feedback mechanism. AI-integrated assessment tools, such as automated grading systems and adaptive testing platforms, provide a seamless way to evaluate student work while offering personalized feedback. These tools use AI algorithms to assess student submissions accurately, highlighting errors and providing corrective feedback alongside scores. For example, in an essay-writing exercise, AI can evaluate the content for coherence, grammar, and adherence to the prompt, providing students with specific insights into areas of improvement. This integration makes the assessment process more efficient and ensures that feedback is integral to the learning experience, not an afterthought. By continuously providing constructive feedback, AI-integrated tools help students see assessments as opportunities for growth rather than mere performance evaluations.

In this AI-enhanced educational framework, feedback is no longer a bottleneck but a powerful catalyst for learning and growth. It transforms the traditional feedback loop into a dynamic, interactive, and highly responsive process that significantly enhances the educational experience. As educators, leveraging these AI tools allows you to provide your students with the immediate, personalized support they need to succeed, fostering a more effective and profoundly empowering learning environment.

7.6 MOTIVATING STUDENTS WITH AI-DRIVEN COMPETITIONS AND CHALLENGES

Educational competitions have long been a cornerstone of experiential learning, allowing students to apply their knowledge in competitive settings that mimic real-world challenges. Integrating Artificial Intelligence (AI) into such competitions can significantly enhance their efficacy by personalizing and scaling the challenges to meet the diverse capabilities of all participants. Imagine a coding challenge where each problem set dynamically adjusts complexity based on the coder's previous submissions or a math league where the questions evolve in real-time, ensuring that all participants are adequately challenged yet not overwhelmed. This adaptive nature of AI-driven competitions levels the playing field and ensures that every student remains engaged and motivated throughout the event.

Designing AI-Driven Competitions

To design an effective AI-driven competition, define clear, measurable objectives that align with your educational goals. Whether it's a science fair, a debate tournament, or a robotics contest, each competition should have well-defined criteria that reflect both the knowledge students should demonstrate and the skills they should develop. The next step is to integrate AI to personalize these competitions. For coding challenges, AI can analyze each participant's coding style and ability, tailoring the difficulty of the problems to push their limits without causing discouragement. AI could provide real-time feedback to participants on their argumentation strategies for debates, helping them refine their skills as the competition progresses.

Incorporating AI requires technical setup and thoughtful consideration of how these technologies impact the learning experience. Ensuring that the AI systems used are transparent and fair is crucial. The algorithms should be regularly reviewed to avoid biases that could disadvantage some students over others. Moreover, the data used to adjust the competition's challenges must be securely handled to protect student privacy.

Adaptive Challenges Based on Skill Level

AI's capability to adapt to challenges according to individual skill levels is particularly transformative. This personalization makes learning more effective by ensuring that students are neither bored with tasks that are too easy nor frustrated by those that are too difficult. In a math league, for instance, AI can analyze a student's previous answers to gauge their understanding and mastery of the topic, then adjust the complexity of subsequent questions accordingly. This dynamic adjustment helps maintain an optimal challenge level, keeping students engaged and motivated throughout the competition.

This personalization extends beyond academic skills to include learning preferences and behavioral patterns. AI can tailor challenges to match each student's intellectual needs and preferred learning modalities, whether visual, auditory, or kinesthetic. This holistic approach to challenge adaptation enhances engagement and ensures that all students have the best possible chance to succeed and benefit from the competition.

Recognition and Rewards

Recognition and rewards are pivotal in motivating students, and AI can significantly enhance how these incentives are implemented. AI systems can track individual achievements and progress, providing personalized badges, certificates, or points students can collect and redeem. This system of rewards not only recognizes students' efforts and achievements but offers tangible goals that keep them engaged. Additionally, AI can analyze the impact of different rewards on student motivation, allowing educators to refine their incentive strategies to maximize their effectiveness continuously.

AI's personalization of rewards goes beyond conventional one-size-fits-all recognition systems. It allows for the acknowledgment of unique contributions and achievements, catering to all students' diverse talents and efforts. For example, in a science fair, AI could recognize the winners and participants who have shown remarkable improvement, creativity, or teamwork, ensuring that every student's hard work is acknowledged and celebrated.

Analyzing Outcomes for Future Improvements

AI's role extends beyond executing competitions to include analyzing their outcomes. By collecting and analyzing data from these events, AI can provide valuable insights into their effectiveness and the areas that need improvement. This analysis can help educators understand what works and what doesn't regarding student engagement, the difficulty of challenges, and the efficacy of different reward systems.

Furthermore, AI can help predict future student performance and interest trends, allowing educators to plan and improve future competitions proactively. This forward-looking approach ensures that educational competitions remain relevant and continue to provide meaningful, engaging learning experiences that meet the evolving needs of students.

These AI-driven strategies for designing competitions, adapting challenges, recognizing achievements, and analyzing outcomes enhance students' immediate engagement and motivation and contribute to a more profound, sustained interest in learning. By leveraging AI to elevate educational competitions, you empower students to excel in academic pursuits and their overall personal and professional development. As we transition from this exploration of AI in competitive and collaborative settings, the next chapter will delve into the future of AI in education, examining upcoming trends, potential challenges, and the overarching impact of AI on educational paradigms. This ongoing journey into AI-enhanced education is not just about integrating new technologies; it's about reimagining how we teach, learn, and grow in an increasingly digital world.

8

THE FUTURE OF AI IN EDUCATION

As we stand on the brink of technological revolutions, the education landscape continually expands with groundbreaking innovations. Picture a classroom as a physical space and an intellectual playground where cutting-edge Artificial Intelligence (AI) technologies such as quantum computing and affective computing transform traditional learning paradigms. These technologies are not merely enhancing the ways we teach; they are redefining them, promising an educational future that is more inclusive, effective, and profoundly transformative.

8.1 EMERGING AI TECHNOLOGIES AND THEIR POTENTIAL IMPACT ON EDUCATION

Overview of Cutting-Edge AI Technologies

Among the most exhilarating advancements in AI are quantum computing and affective computing. Quantum computing, known for its potential to process complex data at unprecedented speeds, could revolutionize education areas requiring large-scale data analysis, such as learning analytics and educational research. Imagine AI systems that can instantaneously analyze data from millions of learners to tailor educational content suitably for each student or to provide real-time feedback to educators about effective teaching strategies and student comprehension.

Affective computing, or emotional AI, opens another fascinating chapter in educational innovation. This technology enables machines to recognize and respond to human emotions, providing a more empathetic approach in academic settings. For instance, AI could detect signs of frustration or confusion in students during an online learning session and could automatically adjust the pace of teaching or offer additional resources to alleviate these challenges. The integration of affective computing in educational AI tools promises to understand cognitive patterns and emotional states, enhancing the support systems for students in virtual classrooms.

Potential Educational Transformations

Integrating these technologies into educational systems promises to transform learning environments and methodologies significantly. Quantum computing could enable the creation of highly complex simulation models that could be used for teaching scientific subjects such as physics or chemistry, providing students with virtual laboratories to conduct experiments that are too costly, dangerous, or impossible in the real world.

On the other hand, affective computing could transform the pedagogical approach by making it more responsive to students' emotional and psychological needs, fostering an environment where emotional intelligence is as prioritized as intellectual growth. This could be particularly transformative in special education, where understanding and responding to the emotional cues of students who may not communicate verbally could significantly enhance learning outcomes.

Challenges and Opportunities

However, integrating these advanced technologies is not without challenges. The complexity and cost of quantum computing systems and the ethical implications of affective computing, such as privacy concerns and the need for emotional data protection, pose significant hurdles. Moreover, there is a profound need for infrastructure that can support these technologies and curricula that can adapt to include them effectively.

Yet, these technologies present immense opportunities for enhancing educational outcomes and accessibility. They offer the potential to close gaps in educational equity by providing high-quality, personalized learning experiences to students in remote or underserved regions who currently lack access to such resources.

Fostering a Culture of Innovation

To harness these opportunities, educational institutions must foster a culture of innovation that embraces technological advancements and adapts to them effectively. This involves investing in technology and training educators to utilize these new tools competently and ethically. It also means staying agile and adapting curricula and teaching methods as new technologies evolve.

Institutions might also consider partnerships with tech companies to stay abreast of the latest developments and to co-create educational solutions that are both cutting-edge and practical. Creating interdisciplinary teams within schools and universities can foster an innovative mindset, encouraging educators from different specialties to collaborate on integrating these technologies into their teaching.

In this era of rapid technological advancement, your role as an educator is not just to impart knowledge but to inspire and equip your students to navigate and shape the future confidently. By embracing these emerging technologies, you are setting the stage for a new era in education that is more adaptive, empathetic, and inclusive.

8.2 PREPARING FOR THE NEXT DECADE: WHAT EDUCATORS NEED TO KNOW ABOUT AI

AI Literacy

As we peer into the next decade, a pivotal shift in educational paradigms beckons you, the educators, to embrace AI and become proficient in its applications and implications. AI literacy, therefore, emerges as a foundational skill that all educators must cultivate. You must understand the operational aspects of AI—how to use specific tools and platforms

—and the underlying principles that drive AI technologies. This knowledge spans understanding machine learning processes, data interpretation, and the ethical use of AI in educational settings.

Educational institutions should consider integrating AI education into teacher training programs to foster AI literacy. This could involve partnerships with technology firms or academic institutions that specialize in AI research to develop courses that are both accessible and practical. Such initiatives help ensure that, as an educator, you are not only informed about the current capabilities of AI but are also equipped to evaluate new AI tools and methodologies that may emerge. Additionally, a focus on case-based learning, where you can analyze real-world applications of AI in educational settings, can bridge the gap between theoretical knowledge and practical implementation. By enhancing your AI literacy, you are better prepared to critically assess how AI can be leveraged to improve learning outcomes and to navigate the complexities of integrating these technologies into your teaching practices.

Professional Development

Looking forward, it becomes imperative that professional development programs evolve to include advanced AI training. These programs must address the technical skills needed to utilize AI tools and foster an understanding of ethical AI use and its pedagogical implications. As AI evolves, professional development must adapt to emerging trends and technologies, ensuring educators like you remain at the forefront of educational innovation.

Such programs should also offer continuous learning opportunities rather than one-time training sessions. This could be facilitated through online platforms that provide ongoing access to AI resources and learning modules, allowing you to learn at your own pace and schedule. Additionally, professional development in AI should encourage interdisciplinary learning, bringing educators from different subject areas to explore how AI can be integrated across curricula. By participating in these evolving professional development programs, you not only enhance your teaching efficacy but also contribute to a broader educational ecosystem that is responsive to technological advancements.

Anticipating Technological Shifts

In an era characterized by rapid technological changes, staying informed about AI trends and developments is crucial. This requires engaging with various information sources, from academic journals and conferences to tech industry publications. Building a professional network that includes AI experts and technology educators can provide you with insights and updates on the latest AI advancements and their potential educational applications.

Additionally, adopting a mindset of flexibility and openness to change is vital. AI technologies can transform educational practices and learning environments in unforeseen ways. Being prepared to adapt your teaching strategies in response to these changes is crucial. This might mean rethinking assessment methods or integrating new AI-driven tools into your classroom. Your proactive engagement in learning about and anticipating these technological shifts ensures that your teaching methods remain relevant and practical, providing your students with a learning experience informed by the latest innovations.

Creating Adaptive Learning Environments

It cannot be overstated how necessary it is to develop flexible and adaptive learning environments that swiftly integrate new AI tools as they become available. This involves creating a classroom culture that is open to experimentation and innovation. Students should feel empowered to try new technologies and teaching methods, supported by school policies that encourage technological adaptation.

Infrastructure plays a vital role in this process. Schools and educational institutions must invest in robust IT systems supporting the latest AI tools, ensuring students and educators can access the necessary technologies. Additionally, adopting universal design principles in curriculum development can ensure that AI tools enhance accessibility and learning for all students, regardless of their learning needs or styles. By fostering an adaptive learning environment, you help prepare your students for a future in which technological proficiency is intertwined with all aspects of life, ensuring they are not just consumers of technology but also skilled navigators and innovators of these tools.

8.3 THE ROLE OF AI IN SHIFTING EDUCATIONAL POLICIES

Integrating Artificial Intelligence (AI) in education is a technological upgrade and a catalyst for comprehensive policy transformation. As AI reshapes educational landscapes, it necessitates reevaluating and redesigning academic standards and curricula to accommodate and maximize the benefits of AI technologies. The inclusion of AI education into standard curricula is becoming imperative. This shift requires a proactive approach to embedding foundational AI concepts across various subjects, preparing students to use AI and understand its mechanisms, ethical implications, and applications in real-world scenarios. For instance, integrating AI into a curriculum can give students the skills to critically analyze AI-generated data in science classes or use AI tools to create art in humanities courses.

The potential of AI to personalize learning experiences and enhance educational outcomes calls for updated educational standards that recognize and leverage these capabilities. This involves setting benchmarks for AI literacy among students and using AI in teaching processes, ensuring that AI tools enhance educational equity and accessibility. These standards must encourage the use of AI to support diverse learning needs and styles, making education more inclusive and effective.

However, implementing AI in education requires significant policy considerations that must be addressed to ensure its effective and ethical integration. Key among these is the establishment of robust data privacy laws that protect student information from misuse. Educational institutions must implement strict data governance policies regulating access to and using student data, ensuring it is used solely to enhance academic outcomes and not for commercial benefits. Moreover, policies must consider the infrastructure requirements for AI integration, such as high-speed internet connections and access to AI technologies, ensuring all students have equal opportunities to benefit from AI-driven education.

Engaging various stakeholders in discussions about AI in education is vital for successfully formulating and implementing these policies. This engagement should include policymakers, educators, students, parents, and the tech community. Each group offers unique insights that can help shape comprehensive, practical, and acceptable policies for all parties involved. For example, students and parents can provide firsthand perspectives on how AI tools affect learning experiences and privacy. At the same time, educators can offer insights into the practical aspects of using AI in teaching.

The global landscape of educational policies related to AI showcases a variety of approaches and best practices. In some regions, governments have launched initiatives to fund AI research in education, supporting projects that explore innovative uses of AI in the classroom. In others, educational policy frameworks have been updated to include AI literacy as a core component of the curriculum. These examples provide valuable lessons on how policies can be structured to foster an environment that supports AI's safe, ethical, and innovative use in education. By examining these global trends, policymakers can adapt proven strategies to their local contexts, enhancing the effectiveness of AI integration in their educational systems.

Navigating the complexities of AI implementation in education requires a balanced approach that considers the technological benefits, ethical implications, and practical challenges. By fostering a policy environment that supports innovation while ensuring ethical standards and equitable access, educational institutions can harness the full potential of AI to transform educational experiences and outcomes. This proactive approach in policymaking will enhance today's learning environments and set a foundation for future educational innovations, ensuring that principles of equity, transparency, and inclusiveness guide them.

8.4 ETHICAL AI USE IN FUTURE CLASSROOMS: CONTINUING THE CONVERSATION

Ethics in AI usage within educational settings is not merely a supplementary concern but a foundational aspect influencing every facet of technology application, from development to daily classroom use. As AI technologies evolve, so must the ethical standards governing their use. The dynamic nature of AI means that ethical guidelines must be adaptable and regularly updated to reflect new understandings and technological capabilities. For you, as an educator, this evolution has profound implications for classroom practices and the responsibility to foster an environment where ethical considerations are at the forefront of technology use.

One of the critical areas where these evolving ethical standards become manifest is in the transparency and accountability of AI applications in education. AI systems used in classrooms must be more effective, understandable, and open to scrutiny by educators and students. Maintaining transparency involves communicating how AI systems operate, the data they use, and the rationale behind AI-driven decisions. For example, if an AI system recommends specific educational content to a student, the student and you should easily access information on why this recommendation was made. This transparency is crucial for trust-building and enabling you to integrate AI tools into teaching strategies effectively.

Moreover, accountability in AI usage means establishing mechanisms to ensure that AI systems are used responsibly and that procedures are in place to address any issues or biases that may arise. This includes regular audits of AI systems for accuracy and fairness and creating channels through which students and educators can report concerns or problems. Your role in this process is vital—you are often the first to observe when an AI application does not function as intended or impacts students negatively. By staying informed and vigilant, you can help ensure that AI tools remain beneficial and safe for all students.

Addressing bias and inequality in AI-driven educational tools is another critical aspect of ethical AI use. AI systems can inadvertently perpetuate or even exacerbate existing inequalities despite the best intentions. This happens, for example, when the data used to train AI algorithms must represent the diverse student populations they serve. To mitigate these issues, examining and refining AI algorithms and the data continuously sets they use is essential. This process, known as 'algorithmic fairness,' involves techniques like bias correction and fairness analysis to ensure that AI tools offer equal opportunities for learning and development to all students, regardless of background.

Developing and adopting ethical decision-making frame-works are indispensable to navigating these complex ethical landscapes. These frameworks provide a structured approach to evaluating the moral implications of AI technologies and making informed decisions about their deployment in educational settings. A robust ethical framework should include principles such as respect for student autonomy, justice and equality in AI outcomes, and benevolence, ensuring AI applications contribute positively to student learning and well-being. Moreover, these frameworks should be flexible enough to adapt to new ethical challenges as AI technologies evolve.

Implementing these frameworks involves not just understanding the principles but also practical training on applying them in real-world educational settings. Workshops, seminars, and professional development courses can be invaluable in equipping you with the skills needed to make ethical decisions regarding AI use. Furthermore, these frameworks should be developed collaboratively, involving input from educators, students, AI developers, and ethicists, to ensure they are comprehensive and applicable across diverse educational contexts. By actively engaging in these discussions and training, you help shape the future of ethical AI use in education, ensuring that these powerful tools are used responsibly and beneficially in classrooms worldwide.

8.5 BEYOND THE CLASSROOM: AI'S ROLE IN LIFELONG LEARNING AND CAREER DEVELOPMENT

In an ever-evolving world, education extends beyond the traditional classroom settings and continues throughout one's life. AI-driven platforms designed explicitly for lifelong learning and professional development revolutionize this educational continuum. These platforms offer dynamic, flexible learning environments that adapt to the needs of adult learners, who often balance their academic pursuits with work and family responsibilities. Through sophisticated algorithms, these platforms can curate personalized learning experiences that align with individual career goals, prior knowledge, and learning preferences. For instance, an AI-driven learning platform can suggest a course on data science to a marketing professional who seeks to delve into analytics, or it can recommend a leadership skills workshop to an emerging manager.

These platforms provide personalized content and support varied learning modalities such as video tutorials, interactive simulations, and collaborative projects, catering to different learning styles and schedules. This adaptability makes learning more accessible and engaging for adults, encouraging continuous professional development and keeping individuals competitive in their respective fields. Furthermore, AI-driven analytics help learners track their progress, identify areas for improvement, and adjust their learning paths accordingly. Educators can support a continuous growth and adaptation culture essential in today's fast-paced world by integrating these intelligent platforms into lifelong learning strategies.

In career development, AI's capability to analyze vast amounts of data from various sources, including job markets, industry trends, and educational outcomes, is invaluable. These AI systems can identify emerging job requirements and skill gaps, providing educators and learners with insights that align educational offerings with market needs. For example, suppose AI analysis identifies a growing demand for cybersecurity experts. In that case, academic institutions can promptly respond by designing courses that equip learners with relevant skills, thus enhancing their employability and meeting the immediate needs of the job market. This proactive approach benefits individuals by providing them with targeted, market-relevant education and supports industries in filling critical skill gaps.

Personalized career guidance is another significant advantage brought forth by AI. Career development is no longer a linear path but a complex journey with numerous possible trajectories. AI can serve as a compass in this journey, offering guidance based on an individual's educational background, interests, job history, and career aspirations. By processing this data, AI can suggest potential career paths and necessary qualifications, help set realistic goals, and connect learners with mentors and networking opportunities. This personalized guidance is crucial in assisting individuals to make informed decisions about their education and career paths, ensuring they are well-equipped to pursue their goals.

Moreover, the impact of AI on adult education is profoundly transformative, particularly in terms of accessibility and customization. Adult learners often face unique challenges, such as time constraints and varying levels of foundational knowledge. AI technologies can tailor educational content to fit adult learners' specific learning paces and schedules, making education more accessible to those who cannot participate in traditional settings. Additionally, AI can integrate practical vocational training with academic learning, providing adults with the skills to understand new technologies and apply them in their workplaces. This blend of theoretical knowledge and practical application is essential in adult education, providing learners with the tools to succeed in their current roles and adapt to future changes within their fields.

As AI advances, its role in shaping lifelong learning and career development becomes increasingly significant. By leveraging AI to enhance educational accessibility, personalize learning experiences, and align education with career pathways, educators can provide individuals with the resources they need to succeed throughout their lifelong learning journeys. This benefits individuals by enhancing their skills and career prospects and contributes to the broader economy by ensuring a skilled, adaptable workforce ready to meet future challenges. Through these efforts, AI transforms individual lives and drives societal progress, making lifelong learning a pivotal element of personal and professional development in the 21st century.

8.6 AI AND GLOBAL EDUCATION: BRIDGING CULTURAL AND EDUCATIONAL GAPS

The transformative potential of Artificial Intelligence (AI) extends beyond individual classrooms, reaching into the global educational arena where it promises to bridge significant cultural and educational divides. AI's capacity to provide scalable and customizable learning solutions is crucial as a catalyst for equalizing educational opportunities across diverse geographic and socio-economic landscapes. For educators and students in underserved populations, AI offers a gateway to high-quality educational resources that were previously inaccessible. These AI-driven platforms can dynamically adjust the learning content and difficulty to match local educational standards and student learning levels, ensuring that the educational material is accessible but also relevant and challenging.

Moreover, AI facilitates the deployment of massive open online courses (MOOCs) and other digital learning models that can reach a broad audience at a relatively low cost. These platforms use AI to manage and adapt the learning experience to cater to the needs of a global classroom, enabling students from different parts of the world to learn together and from each other. This scalability ensures that educational resources are more evenly distributed, mitigating the disparities caused by economic constraints and geographical isolation.

Cross-Cultural Learning Experiences

In addition to addressing educational inequities, AI profoundly enriches cross-cultural learning experiences. By integrating AI into educational systems, institutions can offer students opportunities to engage with diverse cultural perspectives, enhancing global competence—a critical skill in today's interconnected world. AI-driven programs can simulate real-world interactions and cultural exchanges through virtual environments where students collaborate on projects, discuss global issues, and share cultural experiences. These interactions foster a deeper understanding and appreciation of global diversities, preparing students to operate effectively and empathetically in diverse settings.

AI also personalizes cross-cultural education by adapting content to reflect the cultural contexts of different learners, making learning more relevant and engaging. For instance, history lessons could be tailored to include global perspectives and locally significant content, helping students see where their stories fit into the broader world narrative. This tailored approach enhances engagement and promotes a more nuanced understanding of global histories and relations.

Language Barriers

One of the most tangible benefits of AI in education is its ability to transcend language barriers. Advanced AI-driven language translation and tutoring tools are crucial in making educational content universally accessible. These tools can instantly translate courses into multiple languages, enabling students from non-English speaking backgrounds to access the same quality of education as their English-speaking counterparts. Furthermore, AI-powered language tutoring systems provide personalized language learning experiences, adapting to the learner's proficiency level and learning pace. This accelerates language acquisition and facilitates better integration into global educational and professional contexts.

These AI systems employ sophisticated natural language processing techniques to translate words and convey cultural nuances, making learning more contextual and culturally sensitive. This capability is precious in subjects like literature or social studies, where understanding cultural contexts is integral to the subject matter.

Collaborative International Projects

AI's impact is most palpably seen in its facilitation of collaborative international projects. AI fosters a global classroom environment where students worldwide can collaborate on projects by providing real-time communication and collaboration, regardless of geographical distance. For example, AI-powered platforms can coordinate project tasks, manage schedules across different time zones, and facilitate seamless sharing and editing of documents. These collaborative projects expose students to international perspectives and cooperative skills needed in a globalized workforce.

Furthermore, AI analytics can evaluate the effectiveness of these international collaborations, providing insights into how different interactions and teaching strategies affect learning outcomes. This feedback is invaluable for educators aiming to optimize collaborative learning environments and ensure they are as productive and educational as possible.

These AI innovations are expanding access to education and actively shaping a new generation of global citizens. By facilitating the seamless integration of diverse cultures and breaking down geographical and linguistic barriers, AI is crafting a world where knowledge and learning are boundless and universally accessible. As we continue to explore and implement these AI-driven strategies, the potential to transform global education into a more inclusive, effective, and interconnected experience grows, promising a brighter future for learners worldwide.

Bridging the Gap to a Connected Educational Future

In summary, the role of AI in global education is multifaceted and profoundly impactful. From offering scalable learning solutions that bring quality education to underserved populations to enhancing cross-cultural competencies and breaking down language barriers, AI is at the forefront of educational transformation. These efforts democratize education and enrich the learning experience, preparing students to thrive in a rapidly evolving, interconnected world. As we move forward, integrating AI in education remains a crucial driver in bridging the global educational divide, fostering learning and a deeper understanding and collaboration across cultures. Looking ahead, the next chapter will delve into the practical steps educators and institutions can take to implement AI effectively, ensuring that its benefits are fully realized in educational settings worldwide.

CONCLUSION

As we come to the end of our exploration of the transformative power of Artificial Intelligence in education, it's essential to reflect on the profound ways AI has the potential to revolutionize our classrooms. Throughout this book, we've delved into AI's numerous possibilities—from personalizing learning experiences and enhancing student engagement to streamlining administrative tasks and bolstering educators' professional development. Each chapter has underscored the capability of AI not just as a tool for efficiency but as a companion in crafting educational experiences that are more inclusive, adaptive, and exciting.

However, as we navigate the integration of these advanced technologies, we must tread carefully, considering the ethical implications accompanying AI. Data privacy, the risk of widening the digital divide, and the potential biases within AI algorithms require our vigilant attention and thoughtful action. Our duty, as educators and leaders, is to ensure that our journey toward technological integration respects the values we hold dear in education—equity, transparency, and integrity.

In this ever-evolving landscape, staying current with AI advancements is not merely beneficial but essential. Maintaining a learner's mindset allows us to adapt these tools responsibly and effectively, ensuring that our teaching practices keep pace with technological changes and harness these innovations to enhance learning outcomes.

To my fellow educators, the call to action is clear. Please take proactive steps towards integrating AI into your teaching practices. Let us not view AI as a replacement for the traditional elements of education but as a complement that can significantly enrich the learning experience. Experiment with AI tools, integrate them into your lesson plans, and observe how they can transform the dynamics of your classrooms.

Collaboration and continuous learning are the cornerstones of successfully adopting AI in education. Engage with your peers locally and globally to exchange insights and strategies for AI integration. The collective wisdom of our global educational community is a powerful resource that can propel us forward. Additionally, I commit to ongoing professional development in AI literacy. As the landscape evolves, so too should our understanding and capabilities.

Policy development and stakeholder engagement are also critical. We need robust policies that support the ethical use of AI in education and ensure that all stakeholders—including students, parents, and educational leaders—are part of these conversations. We can create a framework that safeguards our values while embracing innovation.

Looking ahead, I am optimistic about the future of education with AI. Imagine a world where every student benefits from a learning experience tailored to their needs, preferences, and aspirations. In this world, education is a gateway to opportunity for everyone, everywhere. This future is within our reach if we harness AI's potential responsibly and creatively.

Reflecting on my journey of writing this book, I am struck by the complexity and dynamism of AI in education. The challenges were manifold, but the revelations were profoundly inspiring. It has been a journey of learning, unlearning, and relearning—a journey I hope you will find as enlightening as I did.

So, let us step forward with determination and hope. Let us embrace AI as an ally in our quest to enrich and transform education for future generations. Together, we can shape an educational landscape that is effective and empowering—an environment where every learner has the tools to succeed and thrive in an increasingly complex world.

Thank you for joining me on this exploration. May it inspire you to embark on your journey of discovery and innovation in education. Together, let's continue to learn, to teach, and to grow.

# REFERENCES

Axon Park. (n.d.). How effective is AI in education? Ten case studies and examples. Retrieved from https://axonpark.com/how-effective-is-ai-in-education-10-case-studies-and-examples/

Liaisonedu. (n.d.). Ethical considerations for AI in higher education: Ensuring fairness and transparency. Retrieved from https://www.liaisonedu.com/ethical-considerations-for-ai-in-higher-education-ensuring-fairness-and-transparency/

Classpoint. (n.d.). Machine learning in education: 10 examples & actionable. Retrieved from https://www.classpoint.io/blog/machine-learning-in-education

Student Privacy. (n.d.). Protecting student privacy: Home. Retrieved from https://studentprivacy.ed.gov/

eLearning Industry. (n.d.). How AI is personalizing education for every student. Retrieved from https://elearningindustry.com/how-ai-is-personalizing-education-for-every-student

Hindawi. (n.d.). Integration of an AI-based platform and flipped classroom. Retrieved from https://www.hindawi.com/journals/sp/2022/2536382/

Times Higher Education. (n.d.). The potential of artificial intelligence in assessment feedback. Retrieved from https://www.timeshighereducation.com/campus/potential-artificial-intelligence-assessment-feedback

eLearning Industry. (n.d.). The role of natural language processing in eLearning. Retrieved from https://elearningindustry.com/the-role-of-natural-language-processing-in-elearning#:.

Riipen. (n.d.). AI cheating in academia: A catalyst for educational. Retrieved from https://www.riipen.com/blog/ai-cheating

Berkeley Haas. (n.d.). Mitigating bias in artificial intelligence. Retrieved from https://haas.berkeley.edu/equity/resources/playbooks/mitigating-bias-in-ai/

Student Privacy. (n.d.). Protecting student privacy: Home. Retrieved from https://studentprivacy.ed.gov/

IRIS. (n.d.). AI and access to education: Bridging the digital divide. Retrieved from https://www.irissd.org/post/ai-and-access-to-education-bridging-the-digital-divide

EdWeek. (2023, August). Beyond ChatGPT: The other AI tools teachers are using. Retrieved from https://www.edweek.org/technology/beyond-chatgpt-the-other-ai-tools-teachers-are-using/2023/08

Axon Park. (n.d.). How effective is AI in education? Ten case studies and examples. Retrieved from https://axonpark.com/how-effective-is-ai-in-education-10-case-studies-and-examples/

Tom Daccord. (n.d.). AI tools for science teachers. Retrieved from https://www.tomdaccord.com/ai-tools-for-science-teachers

Stanford HAI. (n.d.). Artists' perspective: How AI enhances creativity and reimagines meaning. Retrieved from https://hai.stanford.edu/news/artists-perspective-how-ai-enhances-creativity-and-reimagines-meaning

Techopedia. (n.d.). Transforming education: AI-powered personalized learning revolution. Retrieved from https://www.techopedia.com/transforming-education-ai-powered-personalized-learning-revolution

Every Learner Everywhere. (n.d.). What is adaptive learning, and how does it work to promote equity in higher education? Retrieved from https://www.everylearnereverywhere.org/blog/what-is-adaptive-learning-and-how-does-it-work-to-promote-equity-in-higher-education/

Midwest Teachers Institute. (n.d.). Twenty-four best AI tools for special education teachers in 2024. Retrieved from https://www.midwestteachersinstitute.org/special-education-ai-tools/#:.

Microsoft News. (n.d.). Educators and students now have a secure AI 'scaffolding' to support them in the classroom. Retrieved from https://news.microsoft.com/source/features/digital-transformation/educators-and-students-now-have-a-secure-ai-scaffolding-to-support-them-in-the-classroom/

Axon Park. (n.d.). How effective is AI in education? Ten case studies and examples. Retrieved from https://axonpark.com/how-effective-is-ai-in-education-10-case-studies-and-examples/

Edutopia. (n.d.). Effective professional development on AI. Retrieved from https://www.edutopia.org/article/ai-professional-development-helps-teachers-tech-integration/

Cornell University. (n.d.). Ethical AI for teaching and learning. Retrieved from https://teaching.cornell.edu/generative-artificial-intelligence/ethical-ai-teaching-and-learning

GovTech. (n.d.). Teachers to train with AI-driven classroom simulators.

Retrieved from https://www.govtech.com/education/k-12/teachers-to-train-with-ai-driven-classroom-simulators

ITN Business. (n.d.). Exploring EdTech trends: The power of AI and gamification in education. Retrieved from https://business.itn.co.uk/the-power-of-ai-and-gamification-in-education/#:.

Frontiers in Education. (n.d.). Impact of virtual reality use on teaching and learning. Retrieved from https://www.frontiersin.org/articles/10.3389/feduc.2022.965640

I3-Technologies. (n.d.). 12 artificial intelligence tools for every educator's classroom. Retrieved from https://www.i3-technologies.com/en/blog/stories/12-artificial-intelligence-tools-for-every-educator-s-classroom/

The 74 Million. (n.d.). How AI can help create assessments that enhance opportunities for all students. Retrieved from https://www.the74million.org/article/how-ai-can-help-create-assessments-that-enhance-opportunities-for-all-students/

HolonIQ. (n.d.). Artificial intelligence in education. 2023 survey insights. Retrieved from https://www.holoniq.com/notes/artificial-intelligence-in-education-2023-survey-insights

Digital Promise. (2024, February 21). Revealing an AI literacy framework for learners and educators. Retrieved from https://digital-promise.org/2024/02/21/revealing-an-ai-literacy-framework-for-learners-and-educators/

UNESCO. (n.d.). Use of AI in education: Deciding on the future we want. Retrieved from https://www.unesco.org/en/articles/use-ai-education-deciding-future-we-want

NCBI. (n.d.). Artificial intelligence in education: Addressing ethical. Retrieved from https://www.ncbi.nlm.nih.gov/pmc/articles/PMC8455229/